The Ripple Effect

It is crucial that each individual seek a form of spiritual practice and belief that is most effective for that individual's specific needs. Through this, one can bring about an inner transformation, the inner tranquillity that will make the individual spiritually mature and warm-hearted, whole, good and kind person. This is the consideration one must use in seeking spiritual nourishment.

His Holiness The Dalai Lama, *In my own Words*

The Ripple Effect

A GUIDE TO CREATING YOUR OWN SPIRITUAL PHILOSOPHY

Anne Jones

PIATKUS

Visit the Piatkus website!

Piatkus publishes a wide range of bestselling fiction and
non-fiction, including books on health, mind body & spirit, sex,
self-help, cookery, biography and the paranormal.

If you want to:
- read descriptions of our popular titles
- buy our books over the internet
- take advantage of our special offers
- enter our monthly competition
- learn more about your favourite Piatkus authors

VISIT OUR WEBSITE AT: **www.piatkus.co.uk**

First published in 2003 by
Judy Piatkus (Publishers) Limited
5 Windmill Street
London W1T 2JA
e-mail: info@piatkus.co.uk

A catalogue record for this book is available from the British Library

ISBN 0 7499 2462 4

Edited by Krystyna Mayer
Text design by Goldust Design

This book has been printed on paper manufactured with respect
for the environment using wood from managed sustainable resources

Typeset by Palimpsest Book Production Limited, Polmont, Stirlingshire
Printed and bound in Great Britain by Clowes Ltd, Beccles, Suffolk

I dedicate this book to dearest Pops, my father – a truly gentle man, who lived every day of his life spiritually.

CONTENTS

FOREWORD

Personal spirituality is a philosophy by which we can access our God and our concept of the divine in our own way, without rules and regulations, without gurus or priests. It needs no temples, churches or meeting houses, and it can be pursued and practised in our homes and our places of work.

This philosophy shows us a way of living harmoniously with ourselves and our fellow humans, the living world and the environment. It shows us how we can be in touch with our soul and our highest aspect. It can enable our spirit to be the strongest and most dominant force in our lives, and it can lead us from fear to peace, through to a state of harmony and balance.

By being 'spiritual' we can be happier within ourselves and, in these days of 'individualism' and solitary living, we can stand alone if we want to. We can live with or without partners or family members and still find inner happiness, peace and contentment.

For the modern day we need a spiritual philosophy that is suitable for a world where we have to be self-reliant and self-responsible; a world where we reject dominance, limitations and controls, and look for our own truths and personal integrity.

This belief system teaches us to take responsibility for ourselves and others by proactively connecting to the divine energies of love and bringing it into our lives and those of anyone who wishes to accept it.

Through sharing and putting the tenets of our belief into action in our daily lives and utilising the amazing powers of the universe, we can fulfil our aspirations of living our lives with love, compassion, understanding and fulfilment, and reach our goal of inner peace, contentment and happiness. As we attain inner peace for ourselves it will positively affect those around us and through the ripple effect it will eventually influence the entire world.

ACKNOWLEDGEMENTS

I would like to thank all the staff at Piatkus, especially Judy and Gill for all their help and support in getting this and my other books out to the readers all around the world. Also to the many readers who have given me encouragement I send my love and thanks.

INTRODUCTION

Someone recently asked me, 'How are you?' and for once I didn't just reply with my stock answer of 'Fine,' but actually thought about it for a moment. That was when the realisation hit me. 'I feel somewhere between great and ecstatic,' I replied. 'And do you know something, I always feel like that these days.' That is the truth of my inner feelings; my level of contentment; my gauge of happiness – the measure of my emotional and spiritual elevation. The person who had posed the habitual greeting question broke into a great smile and said, 'Wonderful. What are you on?'

It was then that I sat down and thought about how I feel from day to day and what it was that had turned my life around. I connected to me (the inner me, that is) and tried to put into words what it was I now experience daily: good feelings, happiness, inner peace. There are no words in our language to truly express these wonderful feelings, surges and moods that have turned me from a person seeking happiness to one who has found it. Why are there no words? Maybe it's because we usually find a negative word to express how we feel, or use a trite and bland 'Fine' or 'OK' that is more of an automatic response than a true expression of our inner state. Maybe there aren't enough of us feeling like 'this' to have a language.

I then started to analyse how I had come to feel this new and constant 'peace' and realised that over the last ten years I had lived to a new credo; a new belief system; a new philosophy. That is, it was 'new' to me. Ten years ago I started energy healing and at that time I began to explore different belief systems for living. I looked into different religions and spiritual philosophies, and studied the emerging spirituality of the day. I started what is widely recognised as a 'spiritual journey' of self-awareness. I recognised the signs of emotional scarring caused by trauma in my past and learned the art of self-healing. I opened my mind and consciousness to encompass my spirit and the spirit of the universe. I spent many hours agonising over the truths of sages past and present, and finding what resonated well with me – what made me feel good. I thought deeply about the reality of God and the presence of God within us all – asking numerous questions of myself and the universe, such as: if God created me then how can he be within me too?

I read books, meditated for hours and discussed the subject with anyone who would listen. In my meditation I found I could open up to other realms of consciousness. There, angels and evolved spiritual beings existed, and I was amazed to find that I could ask questions and get answers that helped me to learn more about life and how it worked.

I began to bring the truths that I discovered worked for me into my daily life, and over time I have developed a creed for my own living. It's not unique and is followed by many people all over the world; people who have chosen to be 'spiritual', to be happy and peaceful. This book is my version of the modern, personal spirituality that is sweeping through the world. If you want to get on a fast track to happiness try and share what I have discovered. You will need to take time to do the inner and healing work, but I hope that I can cut some corners for you in your personal search for answers, and help you to find a way that is accessible and comparatively easy to achieve. I encourage you to take pen and paper – or better still a small book. As you journey with me, note down what feels good for you so that you can create your own life manual, your own guidebook.

Before I start to tell you more about my journey I would like to share with you a dream I had some years ago.

I was climbing a mountain and it was hard. There were paths marked out on the mountainside and stakes had been set into the rock to help people climb, but I was determined to find my own way. The set paths had minders who insisted that climbers kept to the defined paths and didn't deviate onto the rest of the mountain. I felt they were too restrictive and wanted more freedom. As I climbed I occasionally used some of the stakes to help me along, but generally I climbed alone. From time to time I stopped and enjoyed the view, resting and recovering from the effort of the steep climb. I was amazed at how far I had come. Sometimes I would slip on shale and fall back to a previous resting place. There I nursed my bruises and analysed where I had gone wrong and what steps I should now take to recover my position. As I climbed I would see others making their way up – some faster, some more slowly. At one point I looked down and saw that there were a number of people beneath me. I felt strong and confident enough to bend down and offer a hand to help the person just below me, and told him how I had got to my resting point. We sat and chatted and I shared my experiences and told him of the techniques and methods I had learned to get me so far. Then I continued on my way. Later I looked back and saw that same person helping others beneath him.

As the vision cleared I realised that it represented my spiritual journey – the climb up the mountain to reach the peace and serenity that is my goal, which is in fact the state for which we all crave. I welcome you on this journey and I will show you some ways of climbing. By adding them to your own experiences and the wisdom that you have accrued through your own life's experiences, you can evolve your own personal creed for living, which I call personal spirituality. Then, maybe even sometime soon, you will find that you will be helping others on their climb.

I discovered that as I worked my way along my path I changed and became more at ease with myself, and generally raised my standard emotional base to that of 'happy'. I realised that those sharing my life – my husband, family and friends – were also affected. As I became 'easier to live with', to quote my husband, so they became happier too. It is obvious that as we transform ourselves there is a spill-over effect – a ripple effect that can influence thousands if not millions of people without any effort on our part. I actually had a vision of this some time ago, which came to me as follows.

After I had been practising energy healing for a couple of years it was suggested that I start to give workshops and show other people how they could connect with the healing energies and pass on all that I had learned. It was at this time that I had a vision of a beautiful lake, with water so still that it looked like glass. Drops of water fell on the waters of the lake, and these created ripples. The ripples went on flowing further and further out as far as the eye could see.

I understood from this vision that you can create ripples in many different ways: by changing yourself; by helping someone; by a positive act that helps the environment; by showing your love for life; by passing on your knowledge and understanding of life. You can affect countless numbers of people, because the power of the ripple effect passes love and understanding gently and slowly through the entire world.

I experienced an instance of this a few months ago when I went to a wedding in London of one of our teachers from Malaysia. The teacher, a Hindu woman, had met a Malaysian Moslem working in London during a holiday here and had fallen in love. They were celebrating the first of their three wedding cere-monies – in a registry office in London, in a Hindu temple in Malaysia and in a mosque.

I was enjoying a meal after the ceremony in London when a young man came up to me. He asked me if my name was Anne Jones and said that he had wanted to meet me for some time as he had a book of mine. At this time my first book hadn't even been published, so I wondered what book he was referring too. He described the course notebook that I had printed for the beginners' healing workshop, and told me that he used it regu-larly and passed it around to his friends at college. Apparently the book had come from someone who had been on one of my workshops in Malaysia, and it had ended up in London – a wonderful example of how the ripples can spread with very little effort.

Remember that every time you smile at someone you start a ripple – the person who receives the smile will feel good and will in turn pass that good feeling to the next person they meet, and so on. Keep remembering how little effort it takes to create ripples in your daily life.

So, let's start a ripple – even your intention to tread this path will begin the process.

My aim is to guide you as you take your journey to discover more about yourself and life in general, and to offer you advice and techniques that will help you in your journey. I will share with you my own personal philosophy, which you can adopt, adapt or extract from until you arrive at a philosophy that resonates well with you. I will also be offering suggestions to show you how you can bring this philosophy into action and use it to help you handle the events and challenges of your daily life. This book can therefore be used as a form of spiritual directory for the extraordinary challenges that this century brings.

Part I

The Journey

THE GOAL

Every man, woman and child has one common goal. Each and every one of us seeks happiness. Many people spend a lifetime looking in the wrong places. The happiness your soul calls for goes beyond the pleasures of the material world to an exquisite feeling of elation and soaring joy. This brings a contentment and peace that calms and suffuses your entire being. Once you find this for yourself it will spread to all those around you and its ripples will affect the entire world.

THE PATH

Every day of your life you experience something that you can use either as a lesson or as a reason to be a victim. If you choose to learn from your life's challenges you can make good progress along the path to your goal; but if you let yourself become a victim you will get stuck and your journey will be painful and slow.

1

Chapter One

STARTING THE JOURNEY

I would like to take you on a journey – the destination is a place of true happiness and harmony. Some people call this a spiritual journey, but let's just look on it as a journey of discovery. The journey will be eventful and perhaps challenging at times, and it will always be amazing.

Before you start your journey I would like to point out that it is not about improving yourself, or about making you 'better'; you are perfectly fine as you are. It's not about good or bad or right or wrong, but about discovering a way of living that gives you a brighter, more uplifting perception of yourself and your world. Through your discovery of inner harmony you will bring a sense of peace and light into the world around you so that people will begin to treat you differently, and life as a whole will become more understandable and less confrontational.

Those around you, who share your life, will also benefit from you taking this trip. For as you discover more about yourself and become happier, your feelings will spill over to those around you. You will be creating your own ripples. It has been said that when a butterfly flaps its wings in Brazil a tornado is created in Texas. Everything we do and every state we are in has an effect on others. Through the ripple effect, the happiness you find will touch the lives of everyone in the world. Moreover, this can be achieved without you getting on a stage to preach or cloistering yourself in a cave in the Himalayas. It can be done within the boundaries of your normal everyday life. All the lessons you need, all the experience you require, all the wisdom and all the knowledge you will receive and draw to you can come from your day-to-day existence.

WHAT CAN YOU CHANGE?

Your goal is to transform yourself, to change yourself to a person who is happy within, who has the peace and calm that seem to radiate from some people quite naturally. But can you change your life? Can you stop yourself from being an angry person? Can you become better off? Can you stop your mother from criticising everything you do? Can you find a job that suits you better? Can you find a partner who truly loves you? Can you improve your marriage? The answer is, yes.

You can change your life, but only if you are prepared to start by changing the way you think and react. My suggestion is that you start by stepping off the path that you are walking on just now by making a conscious decision to put to one side all your preconceptions, your beliefs, your indoctrination, your dislikes and likes, your attitudes. Deliberately decide to explore another way – another way of being; another way of thinking about yourself and the world. Open your mind and be prepared to see life from a different perspective. I'm not suggesting that you should give up all your beliefs and understandings of life, just that you be open and prepared to accept new ones. For only by opening your consciousness to new ideas and concepts can you travel a new path, grow and develop, and ultimately reach your goal.

YOUR GUIDE

It is my belief that you can only really learn from your own experiences. You can, however, find guidance and short cuts by reading about or listening to the experiences of others and their interpretations of what these experiences have taught them. I would like to be a guide for you as you travel this path. To introduce myself to you and therefore add some validity to what you are about to read, let me give you a short overview of my life.

As I write this book I am 57 years old. I actually feel somewhere around 40, and although I often think that something must have gone wrong with my calculations, birth certificate and more importantly an octogenarian mother cannot be disputed! I am married to Tony and am currently dividing my life between Hong Kong and Burley, in England, as Tony is a businessman whose work has brought us to Asia – not for the first time.

My parents brought me up in Putney, a suburb on the outskirts of London, and all was well in my life despite the traumas of unemployment and money problems that my parents experienced. My parents loved me very much and fortunately for me were able to show me their feelings constantly. We were a small but happy family unit.

When I was 15 my parents dropped what they considered to be a bombshell on me by telling me that my biological father had left my mother when I was born and I had been brought up by my stepfather. Although this was not a problem for me it caused them great heartache, and this taught me an early lesson on the harm secrecy and holding back feelings and truths can bring. I was delighted with my dear father and found no reason to stop feeling that way, but he and my mother had been hurting themselves for years through worrying and fear that I would reject him.

At 22 – quite young by today's standards – I married a great guy also coincidently called Tony. I lost my only real chance of having a baby when I contracted rubella (German measles), an experience that was painful at the time but which I now view as a blessing considering the way my life has turned out. It was an illustration of how events that seem ghastly at the time they happen can give us something quite special in the long term. I couldn't have achieved everything I have if I had had a family, and I also have an understanding of how it feels to lose a pregnancy and to want children but never give birth. After four years of difficult marriage we went our separate ways with all the pain and hurt that a broken relationship brings.

I became involved with my career, which at that time was in the budding computer business. Yes, I have worked on computers housed in a room the size of a small ballroom and yes, I was around when they were driven by valves! Maybe they are right about me being 57 after all. I met my current husband way back then, but due to the fact that he had a family we didn't get together until 15 years ago, when we met for the second time and subsequently married.

I enjoyed my 15-odd years as a single woman travelling the world in the course of my work, which involved selling computers in far and remote places. I tried a couple of other jobs that proved either unsuitable or disastrous, and learned how hard life can be when you do not enjoy your work. I cannot say that I was particularly spiritual in my beliefs during this time, although I had an awareness of such phenomena as spirits in houses that was to prove useful later on.

I had what I called a fatalistic attitude to life based on the belief that if something bad happened there was probably a reason for it, and that one should move on without dwelling on the past too much. I still think this way today, although I have explored this further and now know that there are no coincidences, just synchronicity, and that the events and experiences of life are our teachers and opportunities to grow. I am also aware that what may seem like disasters at the time can turn into assets. For example, many of the more traumatic and painful events in my life have given me a greater empathy for others and a deeper understanding of the pain that emotional loss and upset can bring.

After my husband and I met the second time, we married and I took on the role of stepmother. That was certainly one of my life's greater challenges – but I shall be talking a little more about this later in the book and will gloss over it for now and move on.

Some years after we were married Tony and I moved to Kuala Lumpur in Malaysia. It was while I was there that I was 'woken up' to the fact that I should be a healer by the exhilarating experience of hearing my dead grandmother's voice telling me to get started and to contact one of the other British expat wives for instructions on how to progress. I approached this person and was amazed to find that she was expecting me – she too had been given a message that I would be starting this work and would be coming to her for guidance.

This experience had a profound effect on me – not just because I heard the voice, which was earth-shattering in itself, but because by opening myself to the possibility and then the actuality of being able to connect to and transfer healing energies to others I unlocked another complete aspect of my self. I opened my mind and my consciousness to an awareness that our spiritual aspect is as important as (if not more important than) our physical, mental and emotional aspects. My friend put me on the right track and gave me some books of Betty Shine to read. I took them away on holiday with me and practised on my friends and family.

When I followed the simple steps for healing that Betty set out in her book I found to my amazement that I could help with the various aches and pains that my 'patients' were suffering – I don't know who was more surprised, my family or myself. I placed my hands on or above the person I treated and they felt relief from their symptoms and told me that they could feel heat passing into them from my hands. Over the years I have added a number of other healing techniques to my sessions, but the method of holding my hands on or above the person is still the basis of my healing.

Energy healing involves connecting to the positive and uplifting energies that flow around us and passing them through to whoever needs them. These energies are generally referred to as universal energies and they can be accessed by everyone. I initiate the process by my intention and the use of visualisation: I envisage in my mind's eye a stream of white light coming down into the top of my head and out through my hands. This may seem hard to imagine but it works! The person receiving the energy can sense the effects in a number of ways. They may experience a feeling of heat, tingling, lightness, euphoria and loss of pain in the targeted area of the body.

Working with healing energies opened the door to the amazing spiritual aspect of our world. The healing worked and I became completely enthralled by this new way of looking at life. From that moment I spent hours reading, meditating and discussing my new beliefs and understandings with anyone who was prepared to join in.

Since then I have dedicated my life to self-healing, self-discovery, healing others and searching for the truth about life. I have had many very exciting and some quite amazing experiences on my journey, and have learned a great deal not only from the events and experiences of my own life, but also from other people's experiences. I have founded two organisations, Ripple – Bringing Light to the World through our own Transformation, and Hearts and Hands – Sharing Healing, Teaching and Spiritual Development. Through these organisations I pass on what I have learned and experienced through seminars, books and other products that align to the philosophy that I have adopted and which I share with you in this book.

WHAT IS A SPIRITUAL JOURNEY?

It is not necessary to change your job, give up drinking, become a vegetarian or buy a ticket to Kathmandu to step onto a spiritual path. All that is required is that you open your consciousness to acknowledging that you are more than a physical being and intentionally aim to connect to the spiritual aspect of yourself, others and the entire world. Healers and mediums are made aware of the spirit in all aspects of life simply because of their gifts and the work they do, but you do not have to have or even develop any psychic powers to be spiritual. There are many paths up the symbolic mountain that we attempt to climb in our efforts to reach inner peace – all religions have the basic tenets that one can use as hand rails – and it is really a matter of finding the one that suits you. I have a belief system and philosophy that suits me; you may decide to adopt some of my tenets along with those of a religion that you were brought up with. This is absolutely fine – it's just a matter of personal choice.

As you begin your journey you will need to acknowledge who you truly are and see what your total make-up is in terms of your energy and your emotional, mental, physical and spiritual aspects. You will also need to start the long process of self-healing that can only begin when you get to know yourself. This can take some time, because as we heal and sort out one aspect of ourselves, so another comes bobbing up to the surface.

You will be releasing the emotions of past experiences and healing the scars, which often manifest as fears, from your past traumas. You will be seeing yourself as a unique and rather special person, and all your issues of low self-esteem and lack of confidence will arise to be helped and cared for. You will spend time for yourself and with yourself, and you will develop self-awareness and start to see the reasons why you react to certain situations and people – why some of those you share your life with press all your buttons!

HOW WILL LIVING SPIRITUALLY AFFECT YOU?

When you live spiritually you make your decisions based on your heartfelt feelings rather than on what you can achieve materially. You look for the beauty in life and the good in everyone, and you search for ways to help others whenever you can. You come to value your life and your blessings, and make an effort to be positive in your attitudes and thoughts. You open your heart and love to everyone, no matter who they are or what they have done – forgiveness is a key word here. You find that you become aware of the spirit of life.

Through your opening consciousness you will begin to connect with the sense of spirit that exists in all living things and spreads throughout the entire universe – this connection can lead to some amazing experiences and revelations. Of course, there will be difficult times as well, as you learn about the deeper and more complex aspects of your nature and being. Sometimes you will feel that you are taking two steps forwards and one step back; there will be great forward leaps followed by some back-sliding, but when you look back you will see just how far you have come. Remember to be patient and be prepared to take tiny steps – I can guarantee that it is worthwhile persisting with your goal.

A JOURNAL

I suggest that you start a journal in which you write down your feelings and the discoveries you make as you travel – a diary of your trip. This will be a log, a record of your progress along your path. Over the years I have collected a pile of these and they are filled with insights and stories, and also with some of the problems and questions that have come up in the course of my journey. Sometimes just writing down problems and queries can help you find answers.

You may also find it helpful to write down your feelings – some of which may have been suppressed for years – as a way of releasing them. As I have already mentioned, one of the most important tasks you will perform on your journey is to clear out the pent-up emotions relating to painful experiences in your past. This is part of the clearing out that you need to do before you can heal yourself and move into the new state of peace, and it is rather like taking off the old wallpaper in a room before redecorating with a fresh new look. You can also use your journal for keeping notes of sayings and ideas that inspire you and any visions or ideas that you may have for your future.

Once these preparations are under way you will have some idea of what to expect, and will probably think that it all sounds like a lot of hard work. This is not really the case, but you will need to apply yourself – but then anything that is worth having is worth putting some effort into, isn't it? Let's now look at who we truly are, and try and gain an understanding of why we are affected so much by our emotions both positive and negative.

I would like to introduce you to a different way of perceiving your complete life form to help you understand why we are so affected by our emotions. Most of our unhappiness and disharmony with life come from the effects of our thoughts and emotions, and they also have a huge impact on our physical well-being. Once you wish to become at peace with yourself you will need to know why you are not peaceful, why you feel uncomfortable with certain people, and why some situations upset you.

In order to understand yourself, you need to accept that you are not just a physical being and to recognise the different aspects that make up your whole. It is also helpful for you to know how these different aspects interrelate. Your spiritual, emotional and mental aspects have huge impacts on your energy and physical state. Because everything you feel, experience and think affects all your aspects, I need to explain these different 'parts' of you in detail.

OUR OTHER BODIES

You will be aware that you have a physical body (that's a good start; an easy one!). You will be aware that you have emotions – those feelings that bounce up at you when you are happy or sad; even if you try to suppress them you are aware of them and their effect on you. You are also aware of the mind, even if you may not be sure where it is and what it actually consists of. (The most common understanding is that it has something to do with the brain. I have my own views on that which I will share with you later.) However, the two other aspects of yourself that you may not be so aware of are the energy and the spiritual sides of your being.

All these different aspects are often referred to as bodies. You therefore have a physical body, a mental body, an emotional body, an energy (or etheric) body and a spiritual body. They are all interrelated, and combined they are generally referred to as the aura. Some energy healers, like Barbara Ann Brennan, have made a study of these different 'bodies' and can sense and even see the different layers that they create within the aura. It isn't necessary for you to know exactly where the aura of your mental body lies around your physical body for you to be able to heal it. It is helpful, though, to be aware that we have these different aspects of our being, and that they do continuously affect all our other aspects and have an ongoing effect on our total well-being.

These various interconnected bodies affect each other all the time. For example, if you are nervous about an upcoming event your mental body will create thoughts of fear, and these will trigger off emotional responses that will manifest in your physical body as butterflies in the stomach, sweaty palms, throat rashes, and so on. You will find that the adrenalin rush that fear produces will either energise you or, if it is severe enough, freeze you with panic. In other words all your 'bodies' will be affected by your thoughts. If, on the other hand, you have a car crash, the physical pain will be remembered. Your mental body will recall it the next time you get into a car to drive and you may find that the fear makes you mentally unable to accept the challenge of driving again.

The connectedness of all these bodies is quite obvious most of the time. One of the problems with modern life is that it moves so fast that we don't allow ourselves the normal recovery time for trauma and we are encouraged to suppress our emotions. This can have long-term effects on our health and mental state, which is why one of your tasks on your journey is to release any feelings that you have stored up. You may, for instance, be holding bitterness that is eating away inside you making you, anxious and stressed, and this in turn could be leading to digestive problems and headaches.

The energy body

The less obvious bodies are the energy body and the spiritual body. Let's first take a look at the energy body. This is the aura, or energy field, that sits around any living particle, whether it's an atom or the entire human body. Even plants, gemstones and water have energy fields. In humans the aura reflects the state of the other bodies – it is in fact really a combination of all the other bodies, as we have spiritual energy, physical energy, emotional energy and mental energy. Your aura can thus reveal the state of your entire being, showing if you are physically sick, mentally disturbed or worried, emotionally upset or spiritually troubled.

Emotional upset is one of the main causes of the disturbance of the entire aura. As a healer I spend much of my time clearing away the effects of emotional upsets that have disturbed the energy body of my patients. Painful encounters and traumatic experience leave scars on the energy body that remain far longer than any physical scarring.

Vibrations

We generally refer to the state of the energy body as being of low or high vibration, to reflect the wavelengths of energy that are pulsing through it. Another way to describe these wavelengths is as positive and negative energy. When we are disturbed or anxious, our thoughts (mental body) create negative energy that condenses into areas of low vibration, which in turn causes blockages. The normal flow of energy around and through the physical body is then disturbed and slowed down by these blocks, and the result of this is a feeling of lethargy or depression, or even physical sickness.

Keeping your energy flow as light and as clear as possible is therefore important for your overall well-being. You need to work intentionally and determinedly towards maintaining a positive attitude in order to avoid the negative energy blocks that we call thought forms from becoming a hindrance to your energy flow. Emotions like anger, fear, hate and despondency all create negative vibrations, and as such will affect the way you feel, especially if they are suppressed. This is why you need to release old negative emotions (*see page 91*).

Positive and negative thoughts

All thoughts create an energy flow, and this energy will reflect the negative or positive levels of the focus of the thoughts. If, for example, you think you are no good or a failure in some way, then the negativity of these thoughts will affect you. Moreover, if you think of someone else in the same way they will receive the energy of your thoughts and will feel the worse for it.

You can use this amazing phenomenon to benefit yourself and

anyone you want to help just by thinking of them and visualising them being happy – your thoughts will uplift their energy and spiritual bodies and give them a 'lift'. This 'sending of positive energy with thoughts' is called distance healing. It is one of the most exciting things that I have learned in my quest and I use it all the time. In fact, Hearts and Hands has a network of volunteers who send positive thoughts on a daily basis to people who are mentally, emotionally or physically sick.

Energy centres

Located on our aura are a number of energy points. These spinning vortexes of energy (they are a little like mini tornadoes) are called chakras, which is a Sanskrit word meaning spinning wheel. They are the points on the body where the physical body and the energy body link. There are a number of these points on the hands and feet and down the centre of the body. They have a significance not only for the physical body but also for the emotional and spiritual bodies. You can enlarge – or open – the spinning circles forming the chakras by your intentions and make their energy centres more effective. The most important chakras are:

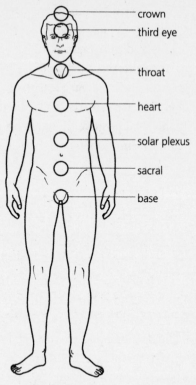

crown

third eye

throat

heart

solar plexus

sacral

base

The chakras

✧ THE CROWN CHAKRA – When this opens you connect
fully with the divine and your spiritual awareness is heightened.
As you make your connection to God this chakra will open like a
great lotus flower, bringing in a stream of the consciousness of
love as a flow of white light. You can use this light to heal all
aspects of yourself, and when it is directed though the hands it
can be passed as healing energy to others. By directing it through
your thoughts you can send a stream of loving healing energy to
others in the process called distance healing. For your spiritual
connection and development you can concentrate on opening this
chakra through meditation (*see pages 19–20, 25 and 56*).

✧ THE THIRD EYE CHAKRA – This is located in the centre
of the forehead, and it affects the physical location of the area

16

around the forehead, ears and nose. It relates to the abilities of visualisation and psychic powers. Visualisation is a powerful tool which you can use to explore your inner self, and it can be helpful in developing your imagination because you can use it not only to connect to spiritual realms and beings – such as angels and guides – but also as a way to see yourself well and happy. The power of visualisation as a tool for manifestation is covered later in this book (*see page 107*).

✧ THE THROAT CHAKRA – As you would expect, this is located on your throat, and it affects the physical state of your upper chest and throat. It influences the way you speak and verbalise your feelings, and is important on your journey because one of the areas we will be working with is your ability to speak up and tell the people who share your life what you really want and feel. Suppressing your needs can be one of the causes of low self-esteem – or, conversely, your low self-esteem can prevent you from speaking out.

✧ THE HEART CHAKRA – This is situated in the centre of your chest and it affects your lungs and chest region and, of course, your heart. When we refer to the heart in spiritual terms we usually refer to the heart chakra. This and the crown chakra are the two most important chakras to open and vitalise on your spiritual path. Your ability to give and receive love is governed by the heart chakra's openness and clarity. If you have been hurt by a loved one or are grieving for someone close to you who has died, this chakra will be damaged and painful. True inner happiness is impossible if this chakra is closed. Your intention during this quest will be to open it through loving, and showing and feeling compassion for, both yourself and others.

✧ THE SOLAR PLEXUS CHAKRA – This chakra is located under the sternum, just below your chest and above your navel. It physically affects and is affected by your stomach and digestion, liver, gall bladder, pancreas and all the other organs in this location.

This is where we store old untreated emotions and where anger and bitterness can be kept bottled up. As I have already mentioned, part of your mission for completeness and self healing is to clear these old negative emotions of fear, anger, grief and hate, and bring in joy, love and feel-good emotions. This is the seat of your power and will, and by clearing away negativity you can use your willpower to enforce any direction you choose in life.

✧ THE SACRAL CHAKRA – Located just below your navel, this chakra affects the rest of your digestive system – your colon and female reproductive organs. It is the seat of your creativity. This creativity is not just restricted to art but is relevant to any form of creation, whether it be starting new projects, recreating yourself as you wish to be, or 'everyday' domestic creativity like cooking or gardening.

✧ THE ROOT CHAKRA – This chakra is positioned at the bottom of the spine and correspondingly at the front of the body. It affects the reproductive organs in men and men's desire to reproduce and initiate sexual relations – so it is the area that sets men's flame alight! The root chakra also physically controls your lower back, your legs and your feet – in other words your support system. If you are feeing lost, unsure of yourself, lacking in confidence or insecure, this chakra is affected. When you move home or job this chakra is the one that is most affected. You can literally be thrown off balance in every respect if this chakra is not aligned.

In your quest for inner light and peace you will find that you will gradually be working your way through the chakras, clearing and releasing them. As you get closer to your gaol, so you will find your body responding more to the upper chakras of the heart, throat, third eye and crown, rather than to the more basic and raw energies of the lower chakras. Caroline Myss has written an excellent book, *Anatomy of the Spirit*, describing this journey through the chakras (*see page 263*).

Each chakra has a different vibration, and there is a colour that has a corresponding vibration – for colours exude energy too, and each one has a slightly different vibration or wavelength.

Below are the colours for the chakras I have described; they are followed by a meditation exercise to assist you in visualising.

Root chakra	*corresponds with*	red
Sacral chakra	*corresponds with*	orange
Solar plexus chakra	*corresponds with*	yellow
Heart chakra	*corresponds with*	green
Throat chakra	*corresponds with*	blue
Third eye chakra	*corresponds with*	indigo – a mix of blue and violet
Crown chakra	*corresponds with*	white

MEDITATION TO OPEN AND BALANCE YOUR CHAKRAS

As I have mentioned, our chakras are most effective when they are fully extended and open, and they also need to be perfectly circular in shape. When you experience a physically, spiritually or emotionally disturbing experience, your chakras can become distorted. The easiest way to heal them is to visualise them in perfect shape. A good exercise to enforce the balance and effectiveness of these energy centres is to visualise spinning circles of colour relating to each centre.

✧ Close your eyes, breathe deeply and relax.

✧ Put your feet firmly on the ground.

✧ Concentrate on your root chakra and visualise a spinning circle of red. See the red disc getting larger and larger and spinning in a perfect circle. This chakra will bring you stability and strength.

✧ Focus on your sacral chakra and see it spinning faster and faster and getting larger and larger. It should form a perfect disc of orange. You will connect to your creativity as this circle spins in front of you.

✧ Think of your solar plexus and visualise a perfect spinning disc of yellow light. Think of the sun and see it becoming larger and larger as it spins. As this chakra spins imagine all your fears flying out of this disc of yellow until the circle gets brighter and brighter.

✧ You now see a green circle of light as you think of your heart chakra and visualise it spinning in the centre of your chest. It becomes stronger and larger as it spins. You are opening your heart to love – to give and to receive.

✧ Now focus on your throat and see a spinning vortex of blue light that spins faster and grows larger until it forms a perfect disc of blue light. You know that you are improving your ability to speak up and state your feelings.

✧ Think of your third eye, in the centre of your forehead, as you see deep violet-blue light the colour of deep oceans. See this colour form a perfect circle that spins wider as you connect with your powers of imagination and visualisation.

✧ Finally concentrate on the top of your head as your crown chakra opens and spins into a perfect circle of white light tinged with purple on its outside edges. As this wonderful chakra opens you become connected to your vision of creation, of God or the greater consciousness that is all. Feel the power of the divine as your crown chakra opens fully.

✧ For your comfort focus on each chakra once more and see each one closing down to a perfect small disc of colour.

✧ Open your eyes. You are now in perfect balance.

The spiritual body

The way we think and the emotions that are created by our thoughts and the thoughts and attitudes of others will affect us spiritually too. Our spiritual aspect reflects our highest aspect. It is our true self, our innermost being, our higher self; it is that part of our being that is most connected to the universal spirit, to the divine or – for some of us – to God. In the section on beliefs later on we will be looking further at the consciousness that some of us call God. Right now I just want you to be aware that you have this very special and unique portion of your make-up that is of the highest vibration and is the part of you that responds to all the positive high-vibration energies of love, joy, respect, recognition, gratitude, compassion, and so forth.

When I share a healing session with someone I am passing spiritual energy to them. It is the highest vibration energy of all, and I leave it to their higher self, their soul, to decide how they will use it. Some people may use it to heal their physical body, some to bring them peace of mind; others will use it to release old emotions and take on an emotional calmness.

Let's now look at ways in which you can connect to the spiritual aspect of your being and the spirit of the world and universe.

Chapter Two

STEPS ALONG THE WAY

Here we look at ways in which we can connect to the spirit of ourselves and all things, and at how we can use these ways to help us move along our path. You will find that you are not alone on this journey – many unseen friends will be watching your progress and guiding you through the difficult times.

FIRST STEP: CONNECTING WITH SPIRIT

Before you can make any progress along your path you need to open yourself and connect to your spiritual aspect. Here are some of the things that will help you to move closer intentionally and open yourself to spirit.

Meditation

One of the best tools you can put in your backpack is knowledge of meditation. Meditation will open you to the realm of spirit, both within yourself and beyond. There are many positive benefits to be gained from regularly practising meditation, including stress release, complete relaxation of the physical body, clearing of the mind and calming of the emotions. The spiritual advantage is that it allows you to connect to your higher self – that part of you that governs your subconscious and connects you to your spiritual aspect.

Meditation will also enable you to go through the gateway of your mind and connect to the spirit world and to the greater consciousness that is the energy of our entire universe. You do this unconsciously all the time in your everyday life through thoughts, ideas, feelings and inspiration, but by using meditation you can consciously free yourself from the constrictions of your physical body and make the connection.

You may already be practising a form of meditation without realising it. When you daydream and let your mind take its own course you are using your imagination to set you free. I see our imagination as the transport system that conveys and translates messages from our higher self, from the greater consciousness that I shall call God and from other spiritual beings that can help us.

Your imagination can therefore be a great asset and certainly shouldn't be dismissed. When I have led meditations in the past people have often said, 'I can't see anything.' But when I asked them, 'Nothing at all – not even some colour?' they replied, 'Oh, but I thought that was my imagination.' It is, but that is the whole point, so let's use this great gift to our advantage.

I favour a form of mediation that is a guided visualisation, meaning that you are guided by someone who leads you through to your imagination, enabling you to open doors to deeper aspects of yourself and to other realms of existence. You can use these visualisations to get to know yourself better, to ask for guidance for your life's issues and challenges, and for self-healing. I have created a CD of the meditations in this book; details on ordering it are included in the Resources section (*see page 30*). Below is a very simple meditation that I first used when I began this process.

GROUNDING YOURSELF

Grounding is a general starting point for all meditations – it relaxes your body and connects you to the Earth. It will stop you from flying off without keeping yourself attached to the reality of your life. If you ground yourself before you meditate you can integrate your spiritual experience into your life.

You can make the experience complete by burning aromatherapy oils – lavender, for example, will be calming and relaxing. See page 28 for an aromatherapy oil blend that will help you to meditate. You can also play soft, relaxing music in the background as you meditate.

✧ Turn off the phones and make sure no one will disturb you.

✧ Make yourself comfortable. Lie down or sit, whichever you prefer. (I prefer to sit as I fall asleep if I lie down.)

✧ Drop your shoulders and relax your body by intending it to go soft.

✧ Breathe in deeply four or five times, and intend that your anxieties and the concerns of your everyday life will leave you as you breathe out. You are breathing in fresh and clear air.

✧ Imagine that you are a great tree and that from the bottom of your feet you have roots that grow into the ground beneath you.

✧ See these roots growing down and down through the layers of the Earth's surface.

✧ See the roots reaching down into the very centre of the Earth. Know that you are completely grounded and centred between heaven and Earth.

MEDITATION TO BRING IN THE UNIVERSAL ENERGIES

I feel passionately that we should be actively bringing in the universal energies: by bringing in the universal spirit you will not only be helping yourself but also lifting the energies of the entire world. In this meditation you will consciously tune in to these energies and intentionally bring them in to enhance your personal energy. White light symbolises the highest vibration of energy, which is emotionally translated as love, so when you do this meditation you will be filling yourself with love.

✧ See a great beam of light coming down from the skies.

✧ The beam of light goes right into the top of your head. There is an energy centre in the centre of your head known as the crown chakra (*see page 16*), and this spins and absorbs the light.

✧ The light now moves into your body.

✧ Feel the light move and intend to take it to every part of your body – through your arms and legs, and into every major organ.

✧ If you are sick or have a pain somewhere, take the light to that spot – the energies have healing properties so see the light staying in that place as it heals.

✧ Know that you are filled with universal love and feel the connection with the universe through this amazing energy.

✧ Just sit for some time focusing on the connection with the universe and letting the light fill every cell of your body and surround you.

Sound

Beautiful and harmonic sound is another wonderful tool for opening yourself to spirit. We often say that our spirits are soaring as we listen to great music. I recently gave a workshop where I wanted to show the impact on clearing negative energies from a room by playing beautiful music and sacred sounds. I was amazed at the effect on the audience – we had some tears and whooshes of uplifting energy flowing through us all.

I find certain music particularly helpful. The traditional *Ave Maria* by Schubert, the *Alleluia Chorus* by Handel and the *Humming Chorus* by Puccini, as well as the themes from *The Lord of the Rings* and *Gladiator* films, are just some of the many pieces of music that make my heart sing, inspire me and open gateways to wonderful energies and feelings. You need to find the music that resonates for you; then, when you want to feel good and open yourself up, turn up the volume and lose yourself in the sound and be transported wherever it takes you. There is no right or wrong choice of music or way to use it – just do what works for you.

Many people also find that sacred chants bring them closer to the divine. I have several recordings by different cultures that have an overwhelming effect on me. The reason they are so powerful is that they are words that have been used for generations to acknowledge God, so they have become sacred and can invoke amazing energies. You might like to try Gregorian chants, which can be deeply moving and may well touch a chord for you. Eastern spiritual philosophies and religions use short verses called mantras that are repeated by monks and devotees over and over again, like the Catholics' 'Hail Mary', and they can create a potent sound and energy for spiritual connection. I find the mantras of Kwan Yin, 'Om Mani Padme Hum', and the sacred chants of Shiva from India, particularly 'Om Nama Shivaya', exceptionally powerful.

Other sounds that may affect you spiritually are those of bells and other objects, such as those used by priests and monks in churches and Buddhist temples. They can send shivers of light energy through you and can be extremely effective in opening you up and uplifting you.

Another, more modern type of sound is one that can come

directly from yourself – namely from your own voice. A friend of mine has been having tremendous success with helping people to relax and let go by running toning circles. The participants just let their voices take them wherever they wish to go. You can achieve this by opening your voice and your throat, releasing your inhibitions and simply singing, letting whatever sound feels right pour from you. Toning can produce some amazing feelings: one of the participants in my friend's group told me that she saw the most vivid and enthralling colours as she was toning. You may wish to wait until everyone else has left the house and then take over the bathroom, where the acoustics are at their best – otherwise your family may have something to say on the subject!

Nature

Those of you who have read my other books will know that I consider a walk in the forest or by the beach a 'cure-all'. The reason for this is that when we are surrounded by natural beauty we can open ourselves to all of creation – we can spiritually reach out and touch this beauty by our appreciation. Gratitude and appreciation have the effect of opening us up spiritually, and when we are in the presence of God's greatest acts of creation and allow ourselves to absorb them we are truly in the presence of the divine. So take yourself off on a trip to the country or the seaside. If you choose to go with a companion, make sure they are the type of person who will appreciate the beauty as you will. The quickest way to dissolve great moments is to be with someone who is cynical or unappreciative.

Perfumes and plant essences

Talking about nature brings us naturally to the subject of the effect of perfumes – not necessarily those manufactured by the designer companies, but rather the perfumes of natural flower essences. The perfumes of pure, aromatherapy-grade plant oils are a real treasure for accessing spirit. Burn them in oil burners or diffusers and drop them into relaxing baths, where you can absorb them uninterrupted and at peace.

The energies of different plants and flowers resonate with different emotional states and ways of being. Plant oils that are particularly good for connecting to your higher self are lotus and frankincense, both essences that will open your crown chakra, and rose, which will open your heart and encourage you into the state of love. I also love the Aura-Soma range of essences, especially the Quintessence 'The Holy Grail & the Solar Logos', which you can dab onto your wrists and then pass through your aura with your hands; it raises my spiritually instantly. If you are interested in these products I suggest you go to their website to find the nearest distributor.

My company Ripples has a range of plant essence oils specifically blended to use for your spiritual journey. The plant essences hold the energies which will assist you to open and connect spiritually.

Loving actions

In this list of ways in which we can connect to spirit and enhance our awareness of our spiritual aspect there is one that I really cannot leave out. It has immense power, and will propel you along your path more rapidly than any other. It also resonates with the energy of the ripple effect as it is a proactive way of passing on your own good fortunes, whether they are relevant to prosperity or wellness, and helping those who are in need.

As I write this I am reminded of a great man I met recently who has spent the last ten years of his life helping the poor of Nepal. He lives and works in the foothills of the Himalayas in the remote villages that are among the poorest in the world. While on a trekking holiday years ago, he noticed that these villages did not have even the most basic healthcare, as a result of which their infant mortality and suffering were among the worst in the world. Mothers had to leave their children unattended while they were working in the fields, and as the villages are perched on the sides of mountains the number of accidents was extremely high. Added to this the traditional cooking source in each village was an open fire at the centre of each of the small mud-and-wattle huts that are the villagers' homes, and many of the children suffered burns and scalds from the fires.

This man was so moved by the plight of the villagers that he felt compelled to go to Nepal and do something about it. He had a small income from his family property investments in London (although he is by no means a wealthy individual) and decided this was enough to sustain him while living there. The initiative that he has started has proved incredibly successful.

He founded a charity called the Child Welfare Scheme Nepal and built a number of day-care centres. There the mothers can leave their children with trained minders who not only look after the children but also provide them with basic healthcare. The scheme has been so successful that after the charity had built ten centres the government of Nepal took on the task and now has plans to build another 1,000 centres throughout the country. This individual has also encouraged the locals to design and build covered ovens that use less fuel, are more effective, send the overpowering smoke and emission out of the house and are safe for the children. His latest project is a vocational training centre and hostel for street children. He is an absolute inspiration and a perfect role model for loving action – and he is also one of the happiest people I have met in a long, long time.

By doing good things for others you create good karma for yourself, and by your kindness you lift the spirits of others. Everyone wins. Such action opens you to your highest level of being and has a profound effect on your most spiritual aspect – your soul. Karma is a word we use for cause and effect and is a universal law, meaning that it works without fail and every-where. No matter how small a kindness is, the effect is always the same: in the long run you also gain. I personally feel that the exhilaration of knowing that I have helped someone is enough.

Another result of giving love through your time, money or attention is that it will open your heart; and to reach your goal of happiness your heart centre will need to be fully open.

SPIRIT GUIDES

Apart from having your own intention to move forwards you are being helped all the time by unseen beings that reside in the world of spirit. They have kindly taken on the task of overseeing your movements, keeping you from danger where possible and guiding you in the right direction (provided they know where you are aiming). Once you have decided to move onto your path upwards, they will be delighted – for they have until now been sending you messages that you may think are just ideas of your own and are probably dismissing. They will be very aware of your progress and will offer you suggestions to make your journey easier. These will most often come as flashes of inspira-tion, but if you meditate you may well be able to make a more direct contact with your guide or guides (we often have more than one), and even have a dialogue with them.

I mentioned earlier that my grandmother had connected with me and urged me to make that life-changing moment, leading me to start healing. I was intrigued with the idea that those who have died and moved on can speak to us. I should point out that her voice came loudly into my head, rather like a strong and compelling thought, but greater. It didn't come through as a sound in the room, although I did look around when I heard her because it was so very clear, and I wouldn't have been surprised to see her by the bed.

I spoke to a friend of mine about this and she told me that she was in touch with a number of beings in the spirit world, some of which are her guides. She said that she speaks to them in her mind and they respond. She also said that this wasn't difficult to do and that meditation helps to get her into a relaxed and open frame of mind.

The next opportunity I had for a quiet moment I went into a meditative state. I took myself into my garden and asked my guide to come there too. I didn't speak out loud (you can if you want to – I find it sufficient to think my messages). Instantly I heard my grandmother speaking again. I have to admit here that some of you may struggle with this. The reasons for this are that you have been told since you were small that imagination is to be dismissed and ignored, and that we are surrounded by people who only believe what they see and are completely out of touch with their spiritual aspect. If, however, you keep on trying and allow yourself to relax into the mood of your chosen meditation, you will find that eventually you will make contact. I have a friend who gets all her messages – just like thoughts and ideas – when she is in the shower. Another friend has long dialogues with her guide while she is driving her car – no, she doesn't have her eyes shut! What is important is for you to be in an open state of mind and relaxed, without the distractions of your daily life.

A few months after meeting my grandmother in my garden I attended a workshop. During the meditation (led by the teacher) my grandmother came to me and said that she was leaving me. She told me she had other work to do and was passing me on to my next guide. I was most upset by this but accepted what she said – I had little choice really. I was then introduced to my next guide, a Native American called Yellow Hawk.

Yellow Hawk told me his nickname was Little Chief. I could actually visualise him in my mind's eye and could see he was huge! Great – a guide with a sense of humour; how wonderful. I rejected him at first, however, because I felt that maybe I had made him up (you see, I also had those doubts about my imagi-nation!), and that it was just too much the fashion to have a

Native American as a guide. He persisted, though, and I felt churlish sending him away, so he stayed and I was gifted with a wonderful teacher who taught me how to use universal energies for healing.

My mother was furious when I told her that my grandmother had gone. 'She can't do that,' she said. 'What could be more important than looking after you?' (My mother has a great attitude towards me and my work but she is a little biased at times!) 'Go and ask her what she's doing next,' she told me. So I had to interrogate my poor grandmother. Her response made a great deal of sense to my mother and calmed her down somewhat. My grandmother had moved on in order to greet and help souls as they arrive in the astral planes (heaven) at the time of their death. She nurses them though the anxiety, fear or emotional pain they bring over with them. My mother was mollified and we both relaxed; this sounded like great work, and as my grandmother had always wanted to be a nurse in her life on Earth it seemed most appropriate.

If you would like some help in connecting to your spirit guide, try the following meditation. I have used it in workshops all around the world and it has proved very successful for many people. Quite recently a medical doctor came to me for healing and during the session he asked me to help him connect to his guide. I talked him through the meditation and he had the most amazing experience. His guide came through as Leonardo da Vinci! He was absolutely delighted and so was I. This was the first time anyone I knew had made contact with someone famous. The next day he called me full of excitement. Leonardo had come through to him and started to channel some fantastic information that he needed in his research into the genetics and treatment of Down's syndrome in babies. I am sure that, given time, he would have found this knowledge, but it would have taken him years of research; here it was handed to him in minutes. Obviously, he will now authenticate the information, but what an amazing experience this was for him!

Most often our guides are far less dramatic, and rarely are they well-known figures. You may have a surprise, though. A woman I guided through a meditation recently to find her guide met a wonderful white wolf – she was absolutely delighted with this 'power animal', as the Native Americans call these animals of spirit. She said he had a beautiful thick coat and was incredibly loving and accessible – not at all like the archetype of a wolf that is aggressive and dangerous. Here is a meditation that will help you contact your guide.

MEDITATION TO MEET YOUR GUIDE

Don't worry if you cannot identify your guide or even see them clearly. It will be enough that you are conscious of their presence, of their existence. It is particularly difficult to see the face of a guide clearly. Have your journal (see page 10) to hand so that you can record your experience afterwards.

✧ Prepare and ground yourself (see page 24).

✧ Ask your guide to meet you in this meditation and give you a message.

✧ See yourself walking along a deserted sandy beach. It is a warm and sunny day with just a slight breeze keeping you at a perfect temperature. Waves are lapping onto the sand and you walk barefoot through the water – it is cooling and refreshing.

✧ You look up and see that the sky is a deep and clear blue. The only sound above the waves is the crying of the gulls as they circle overhead.

✧ As you look into the far distance you are suddenly aware of a figure that is slowly making its way towards you.

✧ You are aware that this is your guide coming to meet you.

✧ As they walk closer you become aware of their clothes. Notice the clothes: you will be able to tell a lot about your guide from them.

✧ Focus on the figure's feet and hands and see if you can make out if it is a man or a woman.

✧ Your guide is close to you now. Do they have something in their hands? This is a gift for you – a symbol that gives you a message.

✧ Ask your guide their name. Is there a spoken message for you?

✧ Spend as much time with them as you wish. When you are ready say goodbye, knowing that you can meet any time you wish. Then slowly leave the beach and come back into your room.

✧ Make a note of your experience in your journal before you forget the details of the encounter.

The Ascended Masters

Some spirit beings are more evolved than others. A group of very highly evolved and wise beings is called the Ascended Masters. They have all lived on Earth for a long time and are dedicated to helping us as we struggle with the problems of life in the twenty-first century, with all its challenges. They want us to become as wise and evolved as themselves, and they are great sources of wisdom and guidance.

Over the years I have connected to a number of Ascended Masters. They have always overwhelmed me with their love, which is so intense that when it comes through I get amazing whooshes and tingles. I am sorry I cannot explain these sensations any other way; they are not normally caused and created by earthly events but come over me when I am in touch with the spirit aspect of life. One of the Masters that I feel especially close to is Kwan Yin.

Kwan Yin

Kwan Yin is a wonderful deity of the Buddhists. She represents the gentle ways of the female and brings grace and mercy. Buddhists have adored her for many thousands of years, and her energy is healing and loving. She acts as a guide for me, and I have been told by many people that they see her in my face when I am healing. I believe that I am a conduit for energy when I heal, so that I do not use my own energy, but healing energies come through me. I transfer my love, but the energy comes from higher forces, universal energies that are of the very highest frequency. The best way I can describe them is that they feel like the greatest love and compassion.

Jesus

One of the most powerful spiritual experiences I have had occurred during a meeting with an old friend on a visit back to Kuala Lumpur. She had come to me for a healing session but before she left she looked up at me and said, 'I have a message for you from Jesus.'

I closed my eyes and I saw an image of Jesus standing before me with his arms and hands outstretched. I felt a great feeling of warmth and tremendous love, and saw him and sensed him stepping into my heart centre. I was completely whooshed from top to toe with shimmers of wonderful feelings of joy and ecstasy. It was amazing. It was particularly wonderful for me as I had rather pushed all thoughts of Jesus out of my mind – I had turned my back on my childhood religious teachings in my quest to find my own spiritual truth. I realised at that moment that we don't have to discard anything that we hold dear.

I must admit that this was the first time I really felt the love of Jesus. Before this experience, everything about him had just been words and stories, and although I had understood the message it had not resonated particularly with me. Now I see his message as one of love and forgiveness. He often appears when I am healing and has said he will bring the people into my life who I need to meet – and they do come, mainly for their own healing, but sometimes to help me, too.

There are many other great spiritual teachers, and some of them allow people who are alive on Earth to act as go-betweens and pass on their messages. This role of messenger is referred to as a channel – the messenger lets a spirit being use their body as a channel through which to pass messages. Some people do this consciously: they get the message in their head and then speak it out loud. Others are what is called trance channels, and they actually allow the spirit teacher to take over their voice box and speak directly.

I have a friend, Helen Barton, who is a trance channel. She works with a Master known as John the Beloved, who was one of Jesus' disciples. John is the most amazing wise and knowing man, and his messages are full of great advice for all aspects of life. What is so wonderful is that he knows everything there is to know about each one of us. It's like speaking to a very ancient and learned family friend who has seen us grow up and also knows what we think. He can also provide insights into the future if he thinks it's appropriate and helpful to do so.

In the new spiritual resurgence that embraces divine and heavenly life forms, these wonderful beings in spirit are closer to our consciousness than before, and we can personally make contact with them through our mediations. I have had amazing help and insights from the Ascended Masters, particularly Kwan Yin, Sunat Kumara, St Germain (who used to be Merlin in one lifetime), Lord Metreyer, John the Beloved and Jesus, who is also an Ascended Master, albeit a very special one. There are books that tell you more about these wonderful beings who have dedicated their continuing existence to helping us, particularly in these difficult times on Earth, and I give details of some at the end of this book (*see page 262*).

Masters and psychics
I would like to make one point while we are looking at spiritual

Masters. I personally am against giving one's power away to gurus or Masters, deities or gods. I believe we should listen to the teachings that appeal and resonate for us, and take advice if we wish.

To slavishly worship and follow every command of another is debilitating and takes away your own personal power. You have to make your own choices, because you are totally responsible for yourself. I have a basic aversion to most of the religions that mankind has created mainly because they are too controlling. The message behind most of them is that you should love and respect yourself and others. However, many religions have evolved into mechanisms that control their followers, and they impose controls and limitations that restrict and inhibit rather than encourage development and expansion.

I believe you should be shedding your limitations, be as good as you can be, be free of fears and inhibitions, love as much as you can, expand and embrace life; that you should be responsible for yourself and make your own choices. Therefore use the access to spiritual teachers and tarot readers, mediums and other psychics wisely. If you are discerning in your approach you can gain immense help from them, and they can be a source of wisdom and assistance on your journey rather than an emotional crutch on which you become dependent.

Angels

Sometimes God uses his helpers in the heavenly realms to answer our prayers and send help when we are in trouble. The best known and most acknowledged of these helpers are the angels. They are God's messengers, and they come in a variety of shapes and forms. A friend of mine saw two standing in her garden; they were about 12 feet high and so beautiful that they left her completely breathless with wonder.

The smallest angels are the cherubim that you see painted on church walls and windows, and the most powerful are the archangels – Michael, Uriel, Raphael and Gabriel. The heavenly realms are filled with these angelic hosts. There is a special angel for each of us who has taken on the role of guardian angel and continually watches and guides us.

Angels possess great light and amazing feelings of love. You may not see them or sense them very strongly, but they are always helping you unseen and silently, smoothing your way and aiding you when you are in danger. Sometimes they appear in human form in order to help someone, and there have been many stories of people who have been helped by angels when they have been stranded and were facing danger, particularly in lonely and wild locations. These helpers generally disappear into thin air after they have been of assistance.

It is sometimes difficult to differentiate between heavenly acts performed by humans and those carried out by angels. I once had an experience during which I received divine help and I am still not sure if my helpers had wings! It came about this way.

Six years ago I had to make a nerve-racking journey from France to Malaysia. I was on holiday in Brittany with some friends. Tony was supposed to be joining us, but I had a call from him from Bangkok, Thailand, to say that he had gone to bed with flu – knowing the temptations of this city I think I was quite relieved that flu was his only bedfellow! On his return to Kuala Lumpur a couple of days later he was still sick, and three days later I had a phone call from there to tell me that he had been rushed to hospital with a suspected heart attack. I was asked if I could get on the first available aircraft to Kuala Lumpur, since the doctors had given him six hours to live!

Fortunately I had discovered Rescue Remedy from the Bach Flower Remedy range, and I administered this to my friends and myself from the moment of the phone call. (I suggest you keep a bottle of this handy; it really helps take away the trauma of a desperate moment.) In the morning my friends dropped me off in Rennes, where I purchased my ticket and caught the plane to Paris.

It's quite a performance changing terminals in Paris and I had a heavy case with me (as I usually do), so I thought I'd better ask for some help (please, angels, someone strong!). Along came a lovely young man who lifted the case onto the inter-terminal bus for me and off it at the other end. Another slurp of Rescue Remedy and I was on my way again.

My next destination was the Singapore Airways information desk, where I found that the charge had not been paid on my ticket. I took another sip of Rescue Remedy and passed over my credit card. The response: 'So sorry, the ticket is over the card limit.' Now what was I to do? There was half an hour left before the flight was due to leave. The young man at the check-in desk knew my story by now and was trying to find some way to get the payment through from Malaysia.

It was a bank holiday both in Malaysia and in France so the banks were closed. I couldn't get at any money and my helper couldn't get an authorisation – another hefty sip, another call to the angels and a large swallow of impending tears! My young man was getting frantic by now; he had run up and down the stairs to the booking office at least six times and I felt I ought to pass my bottle over to him. There were now ten minutes left before take-off and he was considering taking my case off the aircraft – more tears imminent, more gulps and slurps, more calls to the angels.

The young man disappeared one more time, and came back this time triumphant. 'Voila, I 'ave the answer,' he cried, flourishing a credit card voucher which I thankfully signed. He had found a cheap access fare that was under my card limit – thank you, God; thank you, angels. He called a colleague to escort me through the maze of the airport and right onto the aircraft, where I collapsed into my seat and then had a jolly good cry (of relief).

During the flight I thought back over what had happened and realised that God had truly answered my prayers – the two young men were angels with or without wings. And when I eventually got to Tony he was slowly recovering from what the doctors had diagnosed as dengue fever. His collapse had been a seizure caused by an extremely low white blood cell count. So when you are in trouble and desperate, remember the angels and remember the Rescue Remedy!

How do you make a connection?

It is not difficult to connect with angels; children do it all the time. You may find that the following meditation will guide you to that other realm where these beings can show themselves to you and you can then see them in your mind's eye.

MEDITATION TO MEET ASCENDED MASTERS AND ANGELS

This meditation will help you to get closer to and connect with these wonderful beings. Remember to ground yourself (*see page 24*) before you start.

✧ Close your eyes and relax.

✧ You are walking along a path leading through woods.

✧ It is a beautiful day and the sun is shining through the leaves of the trees, creating ripples of sunshine on the path ahead of you.

✧ You keep walking and eventually come out of the woods as the path leads up. You are now walking in open countryside.

✧ You are climbing now, going higher and higher, and you come to the top of the hill.

✧ As you stand there looking over the beautiful countryside that is laid out beneath you, a beam of sunshine suddenly strikes the ground in front of you.

✧ As you look at this wonderful golden beam of light it turns into a staircase that leads up into the sky.

✧ You climb the golden stairs and go high up into the clouds.

✧ You see above you a golden temple.

✧ At the top of the stairs an angel is waiting for you. Make your connection – ask for their name.

✧ The angel leads you into the temple – this is a temple of light and healing.

✧ You follow through to a huge hall, which is filled with a round table at which sit many elderly men and women dressed in white. These are the elders and they are waiting to meet you. They are full of love for you.

✧ You can ask these wise and evolved spiritual beings any question you like. The answer will come straight into your head just like a thought.

✧ Take your time in the temple hall. Ask for the names of the Masters and ask all the questions you wish.

✧ Now your angel is approaching you with a gift.

✧ Take the gift and follow the angel back to the stairs – say your farewells. Descend the golden stairs; come back through the clouds and down to Earth.

✧ Walk back through the woods and back into the room.

Contemplate the gift that you have received and see the symbolism within it. There will be some message or significance that will have a meaning just for you. If you find it difficult to understand the purpose, just accept it and write a note about it in your journal. You may find that the answer will come to you at a later date.

Some years ago I was given a microphone in my meditation and I thought that perhaps this meant that I was going to lose my voice! Soon afterwards I was asked to speak at a large conference. As I stood on the stage and was handed a mike I remembered my angel gift and knew that the angels were with me giving me confidence and courage. Other people I know who have done similar meditations have received crystals, wands, books and flowers – some they understood the significance of, others they just accepted with thanks.

Not only do we receive help from the spiritual realms, but we also get a lot of help from people who are part of our lives. Everything that happens to you is actually a learning experience designed specifically to help you evolve. It might take some time before you can completely accept this, but that's how it is. This understanding is part of the belief system that can give you some answers to the reasons why things happen the way they do, and other questions you may have about life. Let us now take a look at the spiritual belief system that I call personal spirituality.

Chapter Three

UNDERSTANDING PERSONAL SPIRITUALITY

I will now give you an overview of spiritual beliefs that will give you a framework for understanding how life works on a spiritual level. I will show you how can bring these beliefs into your daily life and make them work for you.

THE PURPOSE OF LIFE

Life is a series of cycles. This lifetime is just one of many in the cycle of your soul's journey. The end of this cycle will come when you have experienced everything you need to experience and gathered enough wisdom to evolve. Everything you learn stays attached to you in your spiritual form and moves with you from lifetime to lifetime.

It is rather like collecting data to create a database. The information in your personal database is integrated with a larger database that is the consciousness of our world; this serves an even larger database that is the universe – that is as far as I shall go for now. All those who live in this world and in this universe are connected by their ability to access this large database. Everything that has happened, everything that is experienced, felt and said, and everything that is thought goes into this database. So humanity evolves and so the wisdom of the universe grows.

Contracts, missions and life plans

Before you are born – when you are in the inter-life, the space between lives – you exist in your spirit form. While you are in this state you spend time considering your past lives and working on plans for your next life. You have the benefit of the experience and wisdom of evolved beings, those who have already been through the mill of life on Earth, who have 'won their spurs' and claimed their masters degree!

With this help and with your own perception you decide what it is that you want to understand and what experiences you need to gain this understanding. You may have a mission – a will to help others in some small or greater way, or a desire to give something special to humanity like great music, laughter or works of art. Or you may come to grow your own database through your emotional experiences. Whatever your chosen course, the next step is choosing your parents. This may seem like a strange idea, especially if you have a difficult relationship with your parents – but we do have to choose our parents because we need the genetic strengths and weaknesses that they will give us.

The conscious part of you that is reading this book is only part of the greater you – the essence that is you. When you are born some of this essence – I call it soul energy – joins with the egg in your mother that has both her genes and those of your father. At this point you become a unique being: the combination of your soul and your genetic inheritance from your parents. Your DNA and your soul experience will create the personality and character that will be a part of you for this lifetime. It is important for the work you have chosen to do and the lessons you plan to learn that you have the appropriate personality and genetic characteristics.

Once you are born the wisdom you have accrued before is unfortunately rather out of reach. This is because when you are born you forget the things that have happened in your past, although many children have some recall of their time in 'heaven' and are more aware of the world of spirit than adults. Unless they have pronounced psychic gifts this recall tends to leave them after they start school and are permanently 'grounded' by our schooling system, which is still based on believing what you see with your physical eyes rather than what you feel. However, the plans you have made and your past experiences will affect your thoughts and your character and work at the level of your subconscious, which is often referred to as our higher, more evolved self.

For practical reasons you need to forget past lifetimes to enable you to get the best from the experience of this time on Earth. If you didn't do so you would constantly be referring back and saying, 'Oh, I've done that so I'll not bother with it again.' You may, however, need to repeat something that you haven't quite got to grips with on previous visits. It's a bit like staging a new version of a play with different nuances and different players.

To explain how this works further – if, for example, you need to experience power, you should be able to use it for the benefit of all, rather than becoming a despot or autocrat who uses the power to feed your ego and gain materially to the detriment of others. You may get carried away with the responsibilities that you have and use your power to ruin the lives of others. After this life you will decide to have another go at experiencing power. This time it will be with different parents in a different time span. You should make a better job of it this time around as you will possess the inherent wisdom from the previous experience. You may even be a little wary of taking a position of power because of fear of how you will handle it. It is possible that you will need 20 or so lives before you are satisfied that you have handled power as well as you possibly can. Do you begin to see now? Each lifetime has a purpose that will unfold as you live your life.

If you think of your life you may find that you fear some things without reason and pick up others so easily that they are second nature to you. Your genetic inheritance will explain some of this, but the main reason for it will be your subconscious memory of your experiences from other lives. You can see this in action in families where there are several children brought up by the same parents in the same way: all of the children have very different characters and likes and dislikes from each other.

> Life is a series of lessons
> disguised as experiences

There is a reason for everything

Nothing happens by coincidence and anything that is remark-able enough for you to notice will have a message for you in some way. Everything happens for a reason and every experi-ence can be turned into a positive one, provided you take note of what it has taught you about life, about people and about yourself. Through these lessons you grow and develop – even though at the time you experience a seemingly bad event you can feel devastated by the trauma of it. There will be times in life when you feel completely desolate, but if you understand that there is a reason for the experience that led to this feeling, and that the outcome will be for your greatest good, you will find it easier to cope. It is in our nature to demand that there be a reason for everything – sometimes it is just a matter of looking for the reason, and sometimes it will become clear in time.

Life's troubles can become our assets

Therefore everything that happens, no matter how big or small it is, occurs for a reason. The universe works entirely on cause and effect and harmonics. It can be helpful for you to look for the reason why something has happened, as it will help you to understand what is going on in your life. If you are traumatised or deeply hurt by an experience, you may be able to understand it better some time after the event. You'll be able to look back and say why a particular route was closed to you, why a specific person left your life, or why a relationship didn't work out in the long term.

Now is a good time to take out your journal. Think back over your life and make notes on all the people who have had an effect on you. Describe what they have taught you; include the major upsets and suffering you have experienced through them and state what insights these have given you about life. What skills and understanding have you gained by your trials and tribulations? Once you see that all your experiences occur for a reason, you will have a new perspective on life. It will start to make more sense. Here are a few examples of how this works.

✧ You were disappointed because you failed to get a job you were desperate for but a month later a much better job turned up.

✧ Your offer for a house got turned down but a perfect house came on the market later that suited you much better.

✧ You went out with a man and he let you down but by then he had introduced you to the perfect partner.

Bad experiences sometimes also serve to open us to compassion and empathy for others. For example, the loss of someone who is close to you may make you realise how painful it is to lose love and give you more understanding of the suffering of others.

Look for messages

To use this belief in your everyday life look for messages in everything. Whether it be a broken appointment, an act of aggression from a work colleague or a disappointment of any kind, analyse it and see if there is a hidden message. Is it showing you something about your own behaviour and therefore a message to look within? Is it a sign that you are going down the wrong track? Are you being blocked in some way? If you are, check that you are making choices that truly suit your feelings and that you are not just doing what you feel you ought to be doing. Sometimes people around you do things that hurt you; they may themselves be going through some issues that are causing them pain and reflecting this on you – in other words, it's their problem. You will, however, find that there will be something for you to learn from this if you look closely.

As previously mentioned, sometimes the answers are not clear at the time something happens, so you may have to just accept it and be fatalistic about it. What you don't want to do is to become a victim of the situation. Know that it will be for your higher good on one level or another, and that you have created the situation for some reason. This is the first step towards accepting responsibility for what happens to you rather than being the victim of circumstance. It is a huge step to take along your path and can take a while to learn.

Look for the lesson rather than the blame

Soulmates

So, you are here to evolve and learn. You are also here to help others, and your primary purpose will be to help other people to evolve. We tend to come to Earth with the same people each time. We call them soulmates, and you can find them among your family and your work colleagues – in fact in any part of your life. They can be distinguished from other people by the level of immediate rapport and the feeling of familiarity you experience on first meeting them.

You may even have married someone who fits your idea of what would seem to be a soulmate, although this is no guarantee that a marriage will last. Your contract with a soulmate may well be to remain with them for a limited period of time, in order to help them learn a lesson, or to give them quality time and love. Maybe you are here to support someone through a difficult time, or to have a child with them, but you may then need to move on and gain further experiences with others. Take a moment now to make a list of those people who you think could be soulmates.

Having established why you have your lifetimes here on Earth let's now look at the beginning of the cycle of the soul. How was your soul created? What is the source of your soul?

BELIEF IN THE GREATER CONSCIOUSNESS, OR GOD

God is formless and shapeless and cannot be seen or touched. So how can we believe in him? To believe in God is to believe in humanity. To have faith in humanity is to have faith in God – we are seamlessly linked spiritually, for we are created from the consciousness that is God.

I am often asked whether you have to believe in God to be spiritual. The answer is, of course, no. But I think it may be helpful to you if I explain my perception of God – you may then find that you do actually 'believe' in God, after all (if you don't already).

To me God is the name we give to the greater consciousness that is the accumulated wisdom and knowledge of the entire universe – in fact of all universes. I will refer to God in the traditional male gender form as I refuse to call God 'it', and he/she is not appropriate either. However, God has a male and female aspect, so I could just as easily be referring to she and Goddess. God is the energy that flows through every single thing – every animal, including humans, plant, rock, planet – and therefore God is All That Is. God is everything. Moreover, God is all-loving and completely accepting – so please let go of those ideas that God is the old man with the long white hair and a stick to hit those that do not carry out his wishes.

God is love

God has only one wish for us: that we love and be loved. That is why God is LOVE. I see everything in terms of energy, and I see God as the purest and highest form of energy. God's intelligence and power are phenomenal – he is, after all, the accumulation of all wisdom, so he must be quite smart. His thoughts manifest and create, and we are a manifestation of God's thoughts. As such we are of God and therefore we are God; we are of his energy and we flow with the energy of God. Within each one of us is the spirit that is God. Our soul is created by God from God. Every plant and every bird has the energy of God. Through this we are all connected, and when we hurt another being through this connection we are in fact hurting ourselves.

God in nature

I see it this way. My body is made up of cells. I am a cell of a greater being – let us call this being humanity. Humanity is a cell of a greater being, the planet Earth and all that live upon her. The planet Earth is a cell of a greater being that is the solar system.

The solar system is a cell of the universe, the universe is a cell of the cosmos and the cosmos is a cell of God. So God is within everything around us. The purest form of God's essence is in nature, which is why we feel so good in woods and fields, on the sea and on mountains – and especially in the places that humans have not affected with their energy. This is why so many early religions were based on nature worship of one form or other.

Ancient cultures were aware of the presence of God and probably had a greater affinity with the power of that presence than most of us do today. Their minds were not cluttered with the domestic and global issues that beset us daily. They could sense the energies that flowed around them from the Earth and the living creatures that shared their lives. Nature-based religions were therefore in fact connecting to God, albeit in an indirect way, and they were not actually 'heathen' as such.

These days many people want to use another name or word to describe God as they are unhappy with the implications of the wrath and retribution associated with the biblical God. Many people have lost faith in the religions of the world, although they still have faith in God. They have therefore adopted other names, such as Source, Spirit, Creator, All That Is, or I AM, to describe this amazing intelligence and force of life that has unimaginable and utterly incredible power and is pure, pure love.

Has God changed?

Let's look at the changing face of God. If we go back to the Old Testament of the Bible we see a God that is vengeful and full of wrath. That is, a God who teaches vengeance – an eye for an eye. Has God changed? I think perhaps our perception of him has.

If you can presume that humanity is evolving – although I know it is difficult to comprehend this when we see the atrocities we perpetrate against other living beings – then your perception of God will have evolved too. In the days when the Old Testament and similar texts were written, mankind was accepting of strong and powerful leaders who showed little mercy to transgressors and needed to be respected by all. These leaders identified themselves with God, hence the portrayal of God as merciless and condemning.

Jesus tried to correct this view in his ministry, but the people of that time were looking for a king and tried to place him in that role. He did not come to be hero-worshipped – he came as a role model, with a valuable message. He taught that God wanted us to love one another whatever the differences in our beliefs, positions in society or race. We would certainly not be in the mess we are in today were we to follow this very simple message.

Whether you believe in the existence of Jesus or God or not, the simple truth is that love is the basis of all spiritual teaching. If every single person in the world opened their heart and loved every other single person in the world, we would be in the state of nirvana, heaven, bliss. It's really very simple – we *can* change the world just by loving. This is how the ripple effect works – I am loving and I love you; you are loving and you love the next person, and so on and on. You may say that not everyone will do this. My answer to this is that it can start with you. You can be a role model to everyone you meet.

> Every single man, woman
> and child wants to be loved

BELIEF IN DIVINE HELP AND GUIDANCE

I have mentioned that there are an amazing number of helpers in this universe waiting to assist you when you struggle. These beings range from angels to the direct hand of God. Sometimes their messages come in prophetic or inspiring dreams, giving us ideas about a direction we can take in our lives or warning us of events to come. We often need the most help when we are making big decisions, and this is when meditating can be most useful. Close your eyes, breathe in deeply for a few moments to calm yourself down and slow your pulse, then just ask for help. This may not come through at the time, but you might find that your mind becomes clearer and a solution to your problem may come to you when you least expect it. You may find that someone comes into your life with just what you need. This could be a friend or a stranger who arrives with the answer to your prayers.

Prayer

There is nothing wrong with asking for divine help when life gets tough, or even if you need a little guidance with what may seem just a small problem. Our heavenly friends need to be asked before they can come into our lives and assist us. They want to help, but they need our permission to do so. You can talk to God at any time; you do not need to be in a church or temple, but can do it in your car on the way to work, in the woods, in your garden, in the jungle, in the middle of the street – wherever you have a mind to. Don't be shy – just speak to him. He will listen and will delegate one of his messengers to come to your aid.

I heard my first story of prayers being answered in my Junior Church School in Wandsworth, London. The headmaster of the school, who became a family friend and who I knew as Uncle Alec, had an interesting background and would enthral us at his assemblies with tales of his colourful past. As a young man he had worked as a reporter in Chicago when it was less peaceful than it is now. He described himself as 'rackety' – living in the fast lane and a bit of a lad! One night he was walking through the streets when he saw a door open on to a room full of light, which he felt compelled to enter. Inside, an evangelist was preaching about the merits of giving one's life to Jesus and renouncing the sins of the city life.

Everything the man said resonated with Uncle Alec. It was a life-changing moment for him. He decided to dedicate himself to spreading Christianity and immediately signed up to become a missionary. He married soon after and, following his training, was sent to China to 'spread the gospel'.

Before the war, China was going through one of its hard times and life was not easy for the young missionary and his new wife. Their first baby, John, was born. Times were hard and they struggled to keep a home together. Communications were poor in the remote part of the country where they lived and one day the money from the missionary headquarters in the United States just didn't arrive. They waited for a week and it still hadn't come. They were now getting desperate – they had no food and baby John was continually crying. One night when they were at their wits' end and could see that their baby was now very weak, Alec got down on his knees and prayed as hard as he knew how, begging God to send them some food. The next day he opened the front door and there on the doorstep was a basket filled with fresh food!

God listens to all our prayers

The dark times

There are times when you may feel that you have been completely forgotten by God. Most of us have at one time or another reached the bottom of the pit of despair. The very darkest hour is sometimes called the 'dark night of the soul'. It is a time when we almost lose hope that life can get better. Have you had such an experience? If you have you will understand why it is so named. If you have not, be prepared for the fact that one day you may well be in this very dark and lonely place. You will feel that everything in your life has been to no avail, that you are no longer loved; your self-esteem will probably be at zero point, and everything will seem grey – all colour will leave your world. There are many causes of this state, but most often it is an accumulation of events that plunges us into this deepest despair. I have been in such a pit a couple of times in my twenties and I never wish to go there again.

As is often the case, some good may come out of your worst moments. This darkest hour can be what you need to force you to search for a meaning to life, and to reach out to the spiritual aspect of life for solace, love and understanding. It can be the defining moment that forces you to strip away any pretence and dissemination, and allows you to see yourself and your situation clearly. It can be the catalyst that will propel you on to your spiritual journey.

When life is moving along smoothly, albeit not fully satisfactorily, you can be tempted to put up with your situation and unthinkingly accept yourself without questioning. It is only when you are driven to the limits of despair that you will revolt and start to question things; to search for deeper meanings to life and a better way to live it. Spiritual teacher Eckhart Tolle has said that his enlightening moment came when he was in his deepest trough; this was when he discovered the power of the present, the peace between his thoughts, which he describes in his book *The Power of Now*.

When I was at my lowest ebb I forced myself to stay alone for a few days to face my fear of loneliness and aloneness. I felt strangely comforted during those few days and didn't feel alone at all. From this experience I realised that while I had my mind and senses I would never be alone – I can be my own best friend and companion. I guess you would call this self-awareness and self-sufficiency, and it has been a useful lesson.

Everyone will have a different experience depending on their need. Hold on to hope and know that life is not terminal, that only the physical form ends and that you are never alone. Face your fears and they will disperse; when you are in the darkest place remember that the darkest hour comes before the dawn. When you are in the 'pit' remember to pray and ask God for help and help will surely come, even if it will be in a way you don't expect. My help consisted of the realisation that I had lost my fear of loneliness. Eckhart Tolle was shown that the present moment is a peaceful place once you surrender to it. You may receive your greatest gift in your darkest moment.

MEDITATION TO CONNECT WITH GOD'S LOVE

When I am in the 'pit' – worried about something or despondent – and cannot emerge from this state, I follow this process. I hope it will help you too.

✧ Prepare yourself for meditation (*see page 24*).

✧ Call in your guides and angels.

✧ See a great beam of light coming from the skies – this beam is coming directly from God and is filled with his love.

✧ See your heart centre spinning like a vortex, a funnel of light, and see it getting bigger and bigger. As it gets bigger so it is filled with a beam of light.

✧ Surrender yourself completely to the love that is filling you.

✧ Surrender all your anxieties and worries to God – know that the future will bring you answers and that all is as it should be.

✧ Let go of all your negativity – your anger, frustration, doubts and fears. Surrender them to the light and see them turning into light as they are transformed.

✧ See a clock with its hands spinning backwards as you go back to the creation of your soul.

✧ Fill yourself with God's love – the love of the universe; the love that was your own creation. Surrender yourself back to the creative love that conceived you as your soul was created.

✧ You are now as one with God, your creator.

✧ Stay with that state as long as you wish.

✧ When you are ready, return to your room knowing that all is well and all will be well.

KARMA – CAUSE AND EFFECT

Karma is a spiritual law, which means that it is inevitable; it is not a perception or interpretation of ideals or beliefs but an absolute. The word karma has been slightly misused, as it has come to mean inevitability in itself; it tends to be used in the context of a negative result of an action or behaviour of an individual or group. Karma is cause and effect in action, and the outcome or the effect can in fact be good as well as 'bad'.

I think back to my days in the science labs at school and remember Newton's balls and all the smutty comments they raised! We set the balls in motion and as they swung one way they inevitably then swung back in the opposite direction; when they where swung against each other they hit and went out and came back and hit again. We all live according to a similar inevitable action. When we do something it will cause some reaction to return to us. If we do something kind and loving, loving kindness will come back. If we hurt another being, something hurtful will come back to us. Every positive action or thought will bring back a positive reaction, and every negative action or thought will bring back a negative reaction.

The outcomes of our actions may not be immediate (although

karma is reacting quicker for us these days due to a speed-up in the evolution of humanity as a whole). The outcomes may not be exactly the same as the initiating action. By this I mean that you may love your husband dearly and unconditionally, but he may not love you back – however, if you let your unconditional love flow to everyone you will receive love in your life even if the source is not the one you hoped it would be. It is up to you to appreciate this love and accept and value it; if you do not you will send out a negative flow and cause a negative reaction.

Eastern religions and belief systems have accepted karma for many thousands of years. Could it be behind the God of retribution of the Bible, the Torah and the Koran? In Christianity Jesus put less emphasis upon karma – he taught it under a different guise. If you love and care for others you will enter the kingdom of heaven. The kingdom of heaven is the state of bliss and contentment that we seek, the prize that awaits us at the end of our spiritual path. This is a positive slant on karma – you give out love so you will receive it. I believe that what you actually receive back is multiplied at least ten times. So, rather than focusing on the retribution and punishing aspects of karma, look at the beauty of the positive returns that will flow back to you because of the love, care, respect and kindness that you give out to others.

> Every kind thought and
> action will be returned

BELIEF IN THE
CONNECTION OF ALL

One day I was driving across the New Forest, an area in south-west England that the kings of old used as hunting grounds. Many of the indigenous oaks were cut down to build ships and as a consequence there are large areas that are treeless now. These swards of open grassland are beautiful open spaces covered in heather, gorse, bracken and meadow, and they are used as grazing grounds by the ponies that roam freely throughout the forest. As I was driving over one of these open areas I had a vision. I stopped the car and watched. I saw a blue fog and from out of this fog came a leaf that then went back into the fog; a horse appeared and then merged back into the fog. Finally, a man stepped out of the fog and then went back into it.

The message I got from this was that the fog was the greater consciousness, the energy that flows throughout the universe; that it is all that exists and that all living things come from this great flow of 'being'. They take a life in a dense form on Earth, and then return to the flow. We are all from the same source and are therefore connected through the substance from which we are created. This 'substance', or energy, is the life force that is called God. The core of the substance is the heart and centre, which is the intelligence and mind of God – the source of all creation. We are all connected – we are individual cells of a larger cell, in the same way as our body is an amalgam of a number of individual cells, which are of the larger cell that is our individual being.

Our connection with everything means that we can be sensitive to the feelings and emotions of others. This can be a problem for us at times. Have you ever walked into a group and felt the tension, or felt the pain of someone close to you even though you are miles away? Twins have this sensitivity at its highest pitch and psychics use it to connect to your greater consciousness – your database – so that they can see what is in store for you.

This connection is one of the great marvels of the world and it is sometimes the cause of some strange occurrences, such as telepathic connections and sixth-sense phenomena. Have you ever gone to pick up the phone to call a friend and they ring you at that precise time? Have you ever known that something has happened to someone who is close to you before you have been informed of it? Later we will be looking at how we can use this interrelationship with others to help with healing and sending help from a distance (*see pages 81 and 119*).

When we become part of a group of any size from two upwards, we actually create a new energy body – a new being. A feeling of belonging starts to rise as soon as we identify with this new body. Examples of this are nationalism at a country level; civic pride at a city, village or community level; friendship and sharing in a small group; teamwork and support in sport and the workplace; clan or gang loyalty; family support, and so on. It is easier to feel the 'oneness' when the group is small, but we all naturally have yearnings to belong and consciously need to be part of a larger being. There is nothing wrong with this. If the world were invaded by aggressive forces from another part of the universe, all of humanity would pull together and become one unit automatically – we would be bonded better than we are at the moment. Unfortunately, we tend to concentrate on our differences and the boundaries between our 'units', instead of looking for our similarities and common goals and working together to improve the well-being of all.

As a spiritual concept of oneness is important in terms of understanding who we are in the bigger picture, we need to be aware that when a single person is in pain, the whole of humanity experiences pain. Looking at this from a positive perspective, as you begin to heal you will be healing the whole of humanity. Once we start to heal ourselves so the whole being will suddenly start to feel better; as in a domino effect, the wellness will rush through the whole being and the entire population of the world will rise in vibration, in feelings of happiness, and joy and peace will be the norm rather than the exception.

Making the connection

How can you develop the feeling of connection to all? You will feel yourself making the connection by opening your heart and visualising yourself embracing the entire planet, loving all without reservation and sensing the core spirit that runs through every one of us and the entire universe – what we call the greater consciousness, or God. By your endeavours to follow the spiritual creed and philosophy, and by working on your own self-healing, you will be helping to heal all that lives. You will feel a natural affinity with those who have similar energy vibrations to you and will draw closer to friends and loved ones who resonate as you do. As we all continue to heal, and as our energy vibrations come more and more into line, we will feel closer to one another, until the day will come when we will all vibrate with the same wonderful energy of love.

THE TRUTH OF DEATH

I started this chapter saying that life is a series of cycles and that when you are in the inter-life before you are born you choose your life's purpose. Let's complete this cycle now and look at what happens when you die.

At the moment of your physical death your soul – the spirit energy that represents your eternal self – leaves your body. There are healers and psychics who can clearly see the colours and form of our energy body with their inner eye (their third eye – the centre of visual and psychic power), and they tell us that our soul is connected to our body by a silver etheric (energy) cord.

While you are alive your spirit body can leave your physical body and go travelling through the many realms of spirit; this spiritual sleepwalking is called astral travelling. You often do this at night when you are sleeping, having amazing adventures that are sometimes reflected in your dreams. You may go on these nocturnal walkabouts to assist people in far and remote places, or to give healing to the planet particularly during times of world crises. Your experiences sometimes leave you feeling quite emotionally and spiritually depleted in the morning. This doesn't explain all your early morning fatigue, but it may be the reason for the occasional feeling you may have that you just haven't had enough sleep, or the vague knowledge that you've left something uncompleted when you are woken by the alarm clock. You need not worry about these night-time trips, as your silver cord will keep your spirit attached to your body and there is no chance that you will not find your way home.

When you die this cord is detached as the need to be connected to your physical body is now over. This allows your soul to move on to the next phase of its existence – to another realm, vibration of life, level of reality, astral plane or dimension, or whatever term you choose to use for the 'heaven' of the Bible. At this stage you will still be very much aligned to the character and personality that you had in your life on Earth, but this tie will slowly disintegrate as you re-establish yourself in your spiritual mode and your higher self becomes reconnected to all the personal wisdom and knowledge that you have accumulated over all your lives. You then become the wise and knowing spiritual being that is your true essence.

Your welcome

Just before you leave your body – or just after – you will see the spirits of those you loved and who have already left the Earth plane before you. They will be your welcoming party! I was talking to someone recently who told me of a wonderful but sad experience she had when her grandmother died.

The entire family were around the old lady's bed when she started to say 'hello' to a number of family members who had already passed away. She had a huge smile on her face and spoke to them so naturally that the entire family were under no illusion that she was in fact seeing them quite clearly. This occurred the day before she died. When her soul eventually left her body she went very peacefully, and her family were consoled with the knowledge that she was with loved ones on the other side. There was not a shadow of a doubt in the minds of all those who had been with her in those last days that her existence was continued in spirit.

So you get a welcome from family members, friends and other loved ones, and also any spiritual teacher, master or deity that you acknowledge on Earth. If you have died traumatically or after severe and painful illness, you will be led to a place of healing. Once you have recovered from your most recent visit to Earth, and the shock of your return if it was unexpected – at least to your conscious human mind – then you can start to evaluate that life.

You compare the mission you set out before your birth with what you managed to achieve; you see how you performed and how you treated yourself and others. There are no judges other than yourself. You will not get a thumbs-down or thumbs-up from a higher being! You will, however, be helped by the evolved beings that act as elders and counsellors as you go through this personal evaluation. You will then take some time to contemplate your progress in the long and careful evolution of your soul and make plans for your next lifetime – your mission choices, intentions and the appropriate parents for your next visit to Earth. So the cycle continues.

The end of your journey

Eventually you will reach a point where you no longer see any advantages in further trips to Earth. This will be when you have learned all the lessons that are available here. Earth is a particularly good training ground because here we have positive and negative energies and all the complex situations these polarities create in terms of human behaviour, attitudes and emotions. We also have the ability to make our own choices, so there is no rigidity or programming to limit our existence (although judging by the way we behave a lot of the time one can doubt this!). We have free will and this gives us great scope.

Eventually, your soul will evolve to the extent where all potential for further development is exhausted. You can then choose to move on to higher realms with whatever they have to offer, or to assist others in their progress by acting as a spiritual Master working with others on either the astral planes or on Earth.

You can go back to previous lives

Many books now exist that explain in great depth and detail what life on the astral planes of existence is like. I have suggested some of these at the back of this book (*see page 262*). They will help you to explore further this aspect of life. It is important that you feel at ease with this concept of life and the continuous cycle of life, as some of the fears and issues you may be dealing with this time around may be linked to experiences that you have faced in previous lives.

Your journey is about self-knowledge and understanding, and you may wish to delve deeper into discovering more about the greater aspect of yourself through a process that is called past-life regression. This is based on the methods psychiatrists and hypnotherapists use in their therapies to find traumas hidden in the subconscious mind that may be causing current difficulties with life. If you have a particular problem that you are dealing with and are having difficulty in understanding the cause for it, a regressionist can take you back to the root cause of the problem in whatever life it occurred.

Harsh circumstances, traumatic events and great suffering can leave scars on our etheric body, and these can manifest in a current lifetime as fears. Just as someone who is burned in childhood may continue to have an ongoing fear of fire throughout their adult life, so you may retain a fear from a past-life experience. The therapist will be able to take you back so that you can find the cause of your fear in this lifetime. After seeing the cause and acknowledging it, you can release it and move on.

I have used this form of therapy on many occasions to achieve a better understanding of myself and to help heal old wounds. I will share one such experience. My problem was that that every time Tony and I went to France I was sick – physically sick. As a result I was very apprehensive of these trips. I must add that French had never been my favourite subject at school; my French teacher positively terrified me, and my oral French had been appalling – I was petrified to open my mouth!

My regression took me back clearly and in great detail to a night-time scene in France at the time of the Second World War. I arrived in a cabbage field in virtually total darkness. I carried a lantern and I was dressed in the blue dungarees that are typical French working clothes even today. I was nervous and making my way quickly to a small copse, where I met up with a dark-haired young woman dressed in the fashion of the 1940s. She was also frightened, and pulled her cardigan around close to keep out the chill of the night and her fear.

We heard the distant sound of an aircraft, and I ran into the field next to the wood and placed my lantern as a signal for the pilot. I was then catapulted into the next scene, where there was an enormous amount of noise as we were chased across the fields by dogs and men in uniform, shouting and blowing whistles.

We were caught, and the next thing I knew I was lying on the floor of a truck with my arms and legs bound; I remember feeling absolutely helpless and was aware of the screaming of the girl as she was beaten by our captors. At this stage I wasn't sure who they were but through the questioning of my regressor I recalled that they were in fact not German soldiers but French police, and they took us both to a police station somewhere near Brest, northern Brittany. I had been attempting to rescue a young Jewish girl and the plane had been coming from Britain to take her and myself to England. It appeared that I was an Englishman working with the local Resistance movement. I remember being very pleased when I realised that the plane hadn't been caught.

The girl was tortured and taken away and I lay in my cell hearing her screams for days. They interrogated me, but treated me slightly better from what I could tell, concentrating on beating me in the stomach continuously. In the regression I recalled little more than that they eventually took me out to the back courtyard of the prison and tied a revolting handkerchief around my eyes that smelled of vomit. My last act in that lifetime was to shout abuse at them for being French (I was quite vocal and used good strong language!) before they garrotted me. I recall being more upset by the handkerchief and the fact that it smelled so vile than my approaching death.

This recollection helped me to clear up a lot of the unanswered questions I had about myself. It overcame my fear of speaking French (well, almost), stopped my sickness while visiting France and explained my fear of having anything placed around my throat – and perhaps the red rash that would appear there when I became nervous.

There are many healers who are trained to help you return to the past. If you feel this is appropriate, I suggest you use this method of healing as a way to discover more about who you truly are – to see the bigger picture of yourself – and also to speed up your search for wholeness and well-being. I would add, though, that this is not an essential part of your journey, and that many people overcome their fears without needing to know the cause.

Having looked at some basic spiritual beliefs let us move on to the aims and aspirations you can adopt in order to live a spiritual life.

Chapter Four

PERSONAL SPIRITUAL ASPIRATIONS

In this chapter we look at personal aims and goals and ways of behaving that connect and bring out our spiritual strength and mastery.

WHAT DOES BEING SPIRITUAL MEAN?

Let's start by looking at what being spiritual actually means. I have already said that to be spiritual you need to accept that there is more to life than the physical. That is the first step. Secondly, you need to raise yourself intentionally towards being a light and loving person. To do this there are some basic spiritual guidelines to follow that show how you can live your life with the greatest consideration for yourself and others. If you follow these guidelines and work on those aspects of your character and personality that are out of line with them you will gradually find yourself changing and attracting lighter, kinder and more considerate people into your life. This will not be an easy task and will be what takes the greater part of your effort and energy on your journey.

> Anyone who intentionally steps onto the spiritual path lives their life with the intent of gaining wisdom and knowledge in order to evolve to the point where they are at total peace with themselves and the world

ASPIRATIONS FOR A SPIRITUAL LIFE

You will see that most of the principles of this philosophy are not new and they are not unique. They are the basics of the code of living that thousands of people from various cultures, races, countries and backgrounds have adopted. Most of them have been the basis of spiritual teaching since Moses passed the Ten Commandments to his people. They create a positive guide for living for the improvement of both your quality of life and that of those around you and, through the ripple effect, the rest of humanity. They form a modern and workable code of practice for anyone wishing to live a spiritual life – and act as a guide on your climb up the spiritual mountain. The ultimate aim is to reach a state of peace within; when we are all in this state, wars will be a thing of the past.

Bear in mind that these are aspirations not laws, and that you will not be able to achieve all of them – some will be easier than others. This will depend on the things you have experienced in your life, the role models you have had and the needs of your own personality and character. Your intentions are not to be a saint, so don't be too harsh with yourself. The days of penance and hell-fire from above are gone, so don't punish yourself if you encounter some difficulties – guilt is not a positive emotion.

There is no particular reason for the order I have chosen for the list of aspirations below. You may feel that some of them have more weight than others; however, to me the first one is the most important of all, and if this one is followed completely I guess the others wouldn't be necessary anyway! Aspire to live your life with:

❖ Love and compassion

❖ Forgiveness

❖ Self-expression and the truth

❖ Self-empowerment and responsibility

❖ Self-understanding and healing

❖ Patience

❖ A positive attitude

❖ Confidence

❖ Self-esteem

I'll now take you through each of these in more detail.

Love and compassion

As a child of the Sixties I can remember the era of flower power and the continuing mantra of love that echoed around the world at that time. It was a time of awakening, a transition from the shadow of the Second World War and the austerity that followed in its wake to a time of liberation of thought; an expansion of our expectations of life, challenging the beliefs and credos of the past. It manifested itself in all aspects of life, including music, sex, art and dress – in fact in every way that we express ourselves. It was the beginning of the Age of Aquarius so we saw the end of the heavy, masculine and controlling aspect of Pisces and the move to the freer, uplifting female energy of Aquarius. We are now well into this new age and one of the significant aspects of it is that we recognise the power of love.

The love I'm talking about here is not the passion that ignites between two people and sets you aflame. Here I'm relating to unconditional love that accepts everyone without judgement; love that is kindness and respect, understanding and tolerance. Unconditional love means accepting people as they are and not becoming aggressive and judgemental just because they are different or are cool towards you. It means showing patience and consideration for everyone you meet, whether it be the street dweller who bothers you every morning on your way to work, or the guy in the office who irritates you with his inane jokes and stupid laugh. Just remember people are the products of their past, so their current condition and attitudes may be caused by intense pain and abuse from their previous experiences.

Love yourself

An important point to note here is that we are talking of loving, respecting and accepting all life forms, including animals and plants, and therefore of respect and consideration for the environment and all creatures. Also of enormous importance is a commitment to respect yourself and treat yourself kindly and with care. Before you can even think of achieving any sort of inner peace and happiness you have to look inwards and see yourself – to look at all aspects of yourself and see the good within and the beauty of your spirit.

Acknowledge all the good aspects of your character and be understanding and tolerant of any damaged or hurting parts of you that may be creating mayhem within. In your journal list all the loving and positive aspects of your character and nature. Write down everything you have achieved, no matter how small;

everything you have mastered – from toddler age upwards. Whenever you feel low in confidence and are struggling with your self-esteem, take out your book and look at this list. Above all be tolerant and forgiving of yourself. I have dedicated an entire chapter to this subject of how we treat ourselves – see Chapter 7.

Respecting and loving all of life

Years ago I visited India on a business trip and was lucky enough to stay in the Taj Mahal Hotel on the tip of the Bombay peninsula (now known as Mumbai). The old wing that had been there since colonial days and was a popular venue for the weddings of rich Indian families was particularly grand. If you have attended an Indian wedding anywhere in the world you will know that these are great events no matter what the fortunes of the family: they are colourful and exciting spectacles.

One day I looked out of my window and saw a procession coming down the street. It was led by musicians, and there were a number of people on horseback. It was a wedding group. The bride and groom and the attendants rode on white horses that were decorated with brilliantly coloured and embroidered saddles, and their bridles shimmered with golden bells. The men and women were also brilliantly dressed. The overall effect was stunning. However, I noticed something that struck me as odd: both the men and the women were wearing masks over their noses and mouths. I asked someone why they covered their faces – was it similar to Moslem traditions? I was informed that they were actually followers of the most ancient religious sect of India, whose spiritual beliefs include the law which states that all life must be protected through non-violence in thought, deed and action. In order not to harm any living thing, they wear masks to avoid inadvertently swallowing or breathing in flies or other small insects.

This is an extreme case of caring for the lives of all living creatures, but I have to say that I would rather err on this side of

caution than accept the rampant wholesale slaughter and careless treatment of animals that goes on in the world – everywhere.
We should respect the lives of all creatures and our living environment. This is one spiritual principle that I feel passionate
about.

I don't advocate that we all become vegetarians – although this
is my personal preference – but the way we treat animals is so
very important for our spiritual development, both individually
and globally. We create negative karma every time we abuse any
animal, whether it be a domestic pet, a wild animal or one bred
on a farm for food. Two of my own pet dogs were rescued from
a breeder who treats her breeding dogs appallingly, giving them
no care or attention, and keeping them in open pens without
warmth or comfort. She uses them solely as money-making
machines.

There are many individuals and companies in the world that
use animals and the environment in this careless way in their
pursuit of wealth. It *is* possible to have a livelihood from the use
of animals, but it should always be done with respect and attention to their needs and feelings. We have to respect and have
consideration for the animals, plants, natural water sources – in
fact anything living that shares the planet with us.

The many aspects of love
The word love has many aspects so if you find the word 'love' too
strong, too powerful or too connected to the emotion you
reserve for your lover, family and close friends, then you may
relate to other words that describe different aspects of love.

CARE
If we care for someone we treat them well; we make sure that we
don't hurt them. We are gentle with them. We are soft and re-
assuring. I see this in the way ambulance drivers and paramedics
treat people. I was knocked down by a truck – very silly of me, I
know – when crossing the road in South Africa some years ago.

I shall never forget the men who picked me up and put me in the ambulance. I was a total stranger and just part of their daily routine, yet they were so sweet and kind, so caring. They spoke to me gently but cheerfully, and they made me feel that everything would be OK and that they were well in control of the situation. They laughed and joked with me. I soon recovered but I was left with the impression of their care for years. When you do kind things for others, especially strangers, you leave a mark on their heart and they always remember you, particularly whenever they are desperate or traumatised by an unexpected situation.

RESPECT

We often use the word respect for those we admire and hold in high esteem. Broadly, however, the word means acknowledging the value of a person's rights of existence and their opinions, and treating them courteously and deferentially. In the past, we were taught to respect our parents. Why was this? Because they have greater wisdom than we do as children, and more experience of life. In order to grow and develop ourselves, we also need to respect ourselves. We cannot completely love others if we do not love and respect ourselves.

UNDERSTANDING

This means making an effort to see the point of view of the other person. If you take time to see the needs of someone, to look for their viewpoint and where they are coming from, you can begin to understand them. Through understanding comes empathy – a connection with the feelings of the other person. With understanding you can find out why the young man in the office is such a bore and a pain. With understanding you can find out what his life has been and why he acts in such an irritating way. You will then find it easier to be considerate of his feelings and will be less likely to mock and deride him for his odd ways.

KINDNESS

When you act with kindness you are putting yourself out for another person. You are making an effort for them. Being kind can be a way of life – an automatic reaction. Rather than say a harsh word say a kind one. Rather than find fault find something kind to say about a person. Smiling goes well with kindness. People who smile a lot are showing the world that they are happy with themselves and what they see around them, and can affect everyone.

We all remember acts of kindness, particularly those of strangers. They often have the most impact when we are hurt or upset in some way – for example, when I first moved to Malaysia I felt very much like a fish out of water; I was rather confused and lost in my new world. I was introduced to Brenda, another expat wife who had been there for about six months and had learned the ropes. She immediately asked me over to her apartment for a coffee. I went to visit her and this warm and friendly act had a huge impact on me. It lifted me up and set me off in the right direction. She has since become one of my best friends. She didn't have to ask me over, but did this as an act of kindness.

My mother still remembers the nurse who was kind to her before she went down to the operating theatre to have a hip-replacement. The nurse came up to her bed and sat on it, took her hand in hers and squeezed it, and told her not to worry, giving her a huge smile. My mother remembers that smile to this day 20 years later.

> An act of kindness is never forgotten

GENTLENESS

This is a softer aspect of love. It reflects the way you handle situations and people. Touching someone gently means you are positively trying not to harm them. The same goes for the way you talk to and treat people generally. I really love this word and what it stands for. I like the idea of gentleness with strength, of being strong inside but using a gentle way to handle life. In my past I often had no time for the soft approach – it seemed to be too weak – but I have learned that there is nothing weak about bringing gentleness into loving; it just needs a level of patience. It's quite easy to get caught up in the rush and push of the fast lane of today's life, with targets to meet in all walks of life, from hospitals to sales' offices, and it is sometimes gentleness that gets left behind when the stress steps in.

> The greatest power is gentle strength

ACCEPTANCE

If you cannot bring yourself to act lovingly in a proactive way, then the minimum you can do is to accept. With acceptance you are at least opening your arms in a modified way. To accept someone is to acknowledge them even if you don't entirely approve or condone them and their beliefs and behaviour. I like the word acceptance because it's quite neutral but has a kindly aspect to it. If you accept someone you are not critical of them, and this is one of the important issues here. We let ourselves down every time we are critical of others. If we look for faults, then of course we shall find them.

So often we can get off on the wrong foot with someone because we make a judgement based on our first impressions –

on what they are wearing and how they look. I'm sure you've made a judgement about someone's character based on their looks, only to find out later that you were entirely wrong (I know I have). After getting to know them better, you've probably found that your opinion of them changed completely.

> Don't judge a book by its cover – it may
> be the best read of your life

TOLERANCE

If you cannot accept someone with open arms you should still find a way to tolerate them. Tolerance means not reacting in any negative way to things that you do not like or approve of. This is a very important aspect of love. It is what is missing in so many parts of our society and, indeed, of the whole world – the ability to disagree with another's views and still let them be. Wars between believers of different faiths have been caused by intolerance. Even today, the radical elements of some religions are arguing and fighting due to lack of tolerance.

I think patience and tolerance go hand in hand. If you can find the time to allow a person to be what they want to be, and to do and believe in the things that suit them, you are acting patiently and tolerantly. Both these principles can be used to great effect in relationships, of course. What we do in our relationships is a microcosm of what is going on in the world. If we love, understand and tolerate our partner, our parents and our children, this can be used as a role model that will reflect throughout the community and hence to the greater environment that makes up our world. Lack of tolerance is a source of great pain and inner turmoil, not just for you but also for the person towards whom you are intolerant. Elsewhere, I look further into the issues of patience and tolerance in our relationships (*see page 000*); they are the keystones to happiness at home and work.

The challenge – disapprove but still tolerate

CONSIDERATION

Through consideration we avoid actions or words that will upset, irritate or disturb the peace of others. In our world at this time there are very large communities living closely together, and it is more important than ever for us to respect a person's space and property. Naturally, we should avoid harming another person's possessions, but we should also have the same consideration for nature and the environment. Inconsiderate people will destroy wildlife, pollute the atmosphere, play their music loudly in the hearing of others, or impose themselves on the time and space of another. Consideration means always thinking of the sensitivities and needs of other people.

We are not the all same – let's value the differences

GENEROSITY

Helping others in whatever sphere – knowledge, time, possessions – is one of the main tenets of spiritual teachings. Life isn't fair; we cannot make it fair or equal but we can do the best we can to help in our own arena. Firstly, you can treat everyone you meet equally in terms of respect, and secondly, you can share what you have with others. I am not suggesting that you need to give away *all* your money and possessions – that is unnecessary, although if that is your wish good for you. For most of us this would be impractical. You can, however, be generous with your time, your thoughts and your knowledge.

Not all of us are prosperous enough to give money, and some of us have little time to spare, but we can all give our thoughts and our love. I am also a great believer in sharing knowledge – as a teacher that is second nature, and I can't understand anyone holding on to information that could be beneficial for others just to make themselves seem superior. We have too much to do to put the world to rights to take this attitude now. As soon as my guides give me some new information and I have tested it and feel comfortable with it, I am compelled to pass it on.

You can do this by telling your friends and work colleagues about all the things you know can make life better – new therapies you have found that work, new teaching that works for you, new products that have improved your life. This doesn't mean you need to preach at people – just let them know; don't be shy to speak out – it may make all the difference to someone.

COMPASSION

I have left this until last as it is my favourite aspect of love and the most important in terms of your own spiritual growth. Compassion always has a tinge of sadness, as through it we connect with those who are suffering in some way. It involves an empathy of souls, a heart connection and an understanding of the pain of another. It is essential for you to work on opening yourself to compassion. Travelling to the places where there are whole cultures who have less than you do is one way of doing this, as are reading, watching television with an open mind and heart (we sometimes get so bombarded with suffering on television that there is the tendency to close down), or working at a hospice or care home. You will have to find the way that suits you and is most accessible to you.

Like most people I have had several lessons that taught me compassion. The most effective experience, and therefore most memorable, came at the end of an incredible heart-opening journey that started in Singapore and ended in Tibet. There isn't enough space to tell this story fully here, so this is an abridged and shortened version. I visited Tibet with a wonderful group of friends. We met up in Nepal, from where we travelled high up into the mountains of Tibet. Due to a number of circumstances, including the tragic massacre of the royal family of Nepal that occurred just before our visit, we couldn't stay for more than a day in Kathmandu. I had little time for orientation and so suffered badly from altitude sickness – in fact I nearly died because of it, and it left me very weak and emotional.

As soon as I was just about back on my feet, we visited a small village and a temple in one of the more remote areas. There was a small boy there who had been badly burned in a fire. His entire face was covered in burns that were still open in some places and still wept. Like the others in our party I gave him some money, and we moved on to visit a waterfall before making camp in a valley away from the dangers of altitude.

That evening I started to get the most incredible pains in my chest. I first thought this was a reaction to the sickness of the previous day, but it persisted and eventually I could feel tingles down my left arm. I became seriously worried and the girls all huddled around me in the tent giving me comfort. We were miles from anywhere, with no phones, and of course no chance of finding a doctor. I asked my guides if they could shed some light on what was happening to me. They told me to relax and that all would be well and that I would live! Although this was of some comfort to me, the pains persisted and my left hand and arm started to go numb.

Then, suddenly, a vision of the small boy on the mountain

came into my mind and I saw his poor dear face again. I felt the pain in my chest getting stronger and stronger, then I just burst into tears and cried for about half an hour as I connected to him and all the children in the world who just need some love and care. The pain went as the tears came, and my heart centre opened as my compassion for the child flowed.

Since then I have done all my healing from my heart, and I feel people's pain and hurt in my chest – not enough to trouble me too much as a general rule but enough for me to feel and understand their pain. Opening your heart to the suffering of others can be a painful experience but a rewarding one too.

Compassion is a total opening of the heart

Of all the great spiritual teachers my favourite is the Dalai Lama. I feel myself welling up just thinking of him – he has a truly profound effect on me and when I see his picture I am overwhelmed with love for him. He is a wonderful role model, showing us forgiveness and compassion. He has forgiven the Chinese for taking his country. This is not just a lip service, for he shows a true absolution and cleansing of all bitterness from his soul. He is a truly great man who is here to show us compassion. He empathises with everyone, no matter what their culture, race or religion. He is an amazing ambassador for spirit. My great dream is to meet him sometime – he is my hero.

Make someone happy
When you take to looking for opportunities to love or to use any of these aspects of love – and there are many more by the way – you will find that you are changing your perspective on life. You

will begin to become more positive and you will also find that people will start to respond to your change in attitude. As you smile and open your heart you will find people smiling back. Take on a challenge – try to make all the assistants in the shops you use smile. I work on the taxi drivers, particularly in big cities – they are a good starting point. You will be surprised at the effect you can have on people.

Another good challenge is to lighten up the lives of the people working in telephone support centres. They certainly need it as most of the people who ring in are already steaming, having gone through the most frustrating invention created by man – the automatic selection of service using your telephone keypad. By the time most of us get to speak to a human we are ready to blow an artery with exasperation. So if you want to do a good deed for the day, use your patience and tolerance and be kind and gentle to the person on the other end of the phone. They will surely appreciate it and if you are still steaming when you have completed your call, punch a pillow or kick a ball to release any further tension. You will find that by changing your attitude you can change the response of those around you, and will have the satisfaction of knowing that you have created ripples.

A little love goes a long way

MEDITATION TO SEND LOVE

If you want to send out ripples without even speaking to someone you can do this by using the energy and the emotions of your thoughts. This is called distance healing. The following meditation will enable you to pass on love without even moving from your home.

❖ Sit comfortably in a quiet place, where you will not be inter-rupted by phones, children or pets.

❖ Relax, close your eyes and make your body as soft as you can.

❖ Consciously let go of your frown and drop your shoulders.

❖ Breathe in four times, deeply and slowly.

❖ See a shaft of light coming down and surrounding you with bright light.

❖ Now imagine another shaft of light like a spotlight on a stage.

❖ See someone you love stepping into that light.

❖ Imagine beams of light leaving your heart centre in the middle of your chest and reaching the person, taking your love to them.

❖ Send packets of love like spinning balls of light that explode all over them.

❖ Saturate them with your love and care.

❖ See them smiling, happy and well. See them at peace. See them safe and secure.

❖ Do this for everyone you wish to send love to.

❖ Finally see the planet Earth spinning in the light.

❖ Gently put your hands to your heart centre and feel the love and sense the light spreading all over your own body.

❖ When you are ready open your eyes.

❖ Take time before you drive or become too active – step gently back into your life.

Forgiveness

Forgiveness is a very powerful and life-changing action. Through the act of forgiving someone you can heal not only them, but yourself as well. It has huge implications and it is difficult. When you forgive someone you give them a great gift, for you allow the pain of a past action to be cleared; to be exonerated. You also give yourself a great gift, because you rid yourself of the heaviness of anger and hatred. When you forgive someone you let go of bitterness and resentment, which are deeply harmful and invasive negative emotions that can burn away within you to the point where they can cause physical harm. Bitterness can destroy your inner peace and harmony more quickly than anything else, and if you live with it for long enough it can destroy your health and your life. Nobody can get rid of it for you – you can only do this yourself.

Forgiveness releases guilt

In extreme cases forgiveness is the release of hatred. It is a truly amazing, beneficial act, and can be a source of renewal. It can also stop an ongoing energy reaction, the destructive swing of a pain-inducing pendulum (you hurt me so I hurt you).

One of the most important things that Jesus came to teach us was how to forgive. He acted as an incredible role model in this respect. He forgave those in his inner circle who turned their backs on him or betrayed him, and he forgave his torturers and executioners and the crowd that looked on without helping him in any way. It is not easy to forgive, especially when you have been badly hurt and wronged.

I had an issue with my biological father. We met for the first time when I was in my thirties, and then we started to write to each other. I really got mad when he stopped writing. One day I sat down and thought it through and wrote a poem to help me release the pent-up feelings. You can also write down your feelings on paper, as if you are writing a letter, and then burn the paper. This is a very effective method of releasing bitterness, which is the first stage of the process of forgiveness, and it always benefits a minimum of two people.

Families are particularly prone to the effects of unforgiven slights and misunderstandings. I have seen entire families split by a past act or words to the point where one member of the family will not speak to another for years. In my own family my cousin hasn't seen her daughter for years because she had a dispute with her father, who has since died. In fact, she didn't even come to her father's bedside when he was dying, or to his funeral. She missed an opportunity to heal a rift that has caused pain to everyone involved. I am sure the split from her parents and grandparents has affected her. I know it has had a devastating effect on them.

By holding on to her grievance against her father she is still hurting her grandfather, who hasn't seen his great-grandchildren for years now. He is 95, living in a home, and suffering from depression, I know that a visit from either his granddaughter or her children would be such a wonderful, uplifting experience for him. We don't know what is going on in her mind and why she has cut off her family so drastically. However, no matter what her reason for this might be, the point is not who is right or wrong – it's a matter of letting bygones be bygones and moving on.

If you cannot understand why someone has either unconsciously or deliberately hurt you or one of your loved ones, consider that your lesson this time on Earth may be one in forgiveness – to learn to let go of the past and to absolve those who have hurt you. No matter how badly you have been hurt, it will be helpful if you can eventually release the pain and forgive.

MEDITATION TO FORGIVE

If there is anyone in your life who you need to forgive, whether they are alive or have passed on, you might find this meditation helpful.

✧ Make yourself comfortable in a quiet room, and loosen your clothes.

✧ Close your eyes and relax; drop your shoulders.

✧ Breathe in deeply four times and consciously relax the muscles of your face.

✧ Imagine that you are a great tree and sense roots growing out from the bottom of your feet.

✧ Spend a few moments letting your roots settle into the earth beneath you, making you secure and stable.

✧ Imagine a shaft of sunlight coming down and surrounding you with bright light.

✧ Imagine that you are standing at the gates of a beautiful garden; you open the gates and walk in.

✧ Close the gates behind you and look around. Let your imagination create the most wonderful garden, with your favourite flowers, immaculate lawns, and surrounded by flowering shrubs and small trees. This is your paradise.

✧ Spend time discovering your garden. Find the natural part where wild flowers grow, find the pool with the fountain playing; as you wander pick a bunch of flowers – take your time.

✧ Choose a bench in your favourite place in the garden and sit down.

✧ As you wait think of someone who has hurt you in the past; someone you wish to forgive.

✧ You will see this person appear before you. They may be indistinct, but just trust that they are there with you.

✧ Spend a moment considering why this person hurt you – maybe they were hurt themselves in the past. Maybe they are jealous of you. Maybe they need love in their lives or they were provoked. Whatever the reason, decide to forgive them.

✧ Walk towards them. Tell them you forgive them and hand them your flowers – a symbol of your forgiveness and acceptance.

✧ Sit back on the bench and see a great beam of light shining down on you from the sky. Sense and feel divine love filling you and enveloping you – imagine you are being wrapped in an angel's wings. Feel the love fill your heart, and sense its warmth fill your chest and spread throughout your body.

✧ Relax in this state for some time.

✧ When you are ready slowly leave the garden, shutting the gate behind you. Know that you can return whenever you wish.

Forgiveness is the greatest gift

Self-expression and the truth

Honesty is an obvious spiritual tenet but it is one that is not always easy to follow, especially when you are placed in a situation where the truth can hurt someone. I am not an advocate of the 'well, it's the truth whether you like it or not; you'll just have to accept it' way of acting – the push it into your face approach. There are usually at least two ways to make a point and the direct way isn't always the most helpful. I think it is useful to find a *kind* way to tell the truth. I am not advocating that you tell lies (even white ones), but I do suggest that you always think twice before you speak.

What is the difference between your truth and your opinion? Your opinion is how you see things, but your truth is related to your emotions and what feels good for you. It is important for you to spend time establishing what gives you happiness and joy, and what disturbs or upsets you. Then, wherever possible, you should move towards the things that strengthen and empower you, and away from situations that trouble and weaken you. It is essential that you declare – as kindly and gently as you can – your feelings to those who share your life.

Here is a simple example of how this works. Penny is married to Pete, who is a passionate supporter of his local football team. Penny has spent the last five years tagging along with Pete to all the team's games both at home and away. She doesn't even enjoy football, so why does she go with him? At the time when they were dating, Pete had been delighted that she'd gone with him to matches; she hadn't had the heart to tell him she didn't enjoy them. She has been going along with her 'lie' ever since, and it has been compounded by the fact that she heard him telling his friends how much she enjoys these outings with him! Then, one day, she tells him that actually she would prefer not to go to the matches. She feels guilty but released. She is now in her truth. Given time she will lose the guilt and all will be well – particularly as Pete is now delighted to be able to go with his friends and have a beer at the pub on his way home!

Personal truths are about your innermost needs and feelings, which you may be tempted to deny. Unfortunately, we are often not honest with ourselves and although this form of dishonesty is not particularly harmful to others it can be quite detrimental to ourselves. If you are forever hiding your own needs you will be slowly chipping away at your own identity as you will be creating a false image of yourself for the benefit of others.

All lies weaken. The inveterate liar will eventually become immune to the queasy inner feelings that most people use as a gauge of honesty. They will be able to look a person in the face and lie, but on one level or another they will be weakened by their dishonesty. You may fool others but you can never fool yourself. I suggest that you start to listen to yourself and see if you are in fact bending the truth at all. Of course, a good story needs some embellishments and you shouldn't become paranoid, but generally speaking you will feel stronger the more honest you are in every aspect of your life – with your family, and in your social and working life.

Lies weaken

Self-empowerment and responsibility

When you are a victim you have no power, no source of correction, no way to reverse your circumstances. This is because you place the power of action in the hands of the person or group who you blame for your circumstances. While you blame someone else for your misfortune you cannot change it. If, on the other hand, you own the problem you can make plans to solve it. This puts you in a far stronger and more powerful position than when you take the stance that outside circumstances or other people are controlling what happens to you. You may, for example, fail an exam and then blame the weather – it was too hot in the room and you couldn't concentrate; blame your teachers because they didn't cover the subject sufficiently; or blame a headache, the neighbours for being noisy and keeping you up all night, the exam board for making it too difficult, and so on.

These 'blames' pass the entire power of passing or failing over to someone else. If, on the other hand, you say that you didn't pass because you were obviously not all that keen to pass – that you didn't care enough to study sufficiently, or had made a mistake in choosing the subject, you can do something about the situation, like studying harder the next time or choosing to drop the subject. Either way, it's down to you.

Of course, other people's actions can be the cause of a problem for you, but if you decide that the only person who can solve the problem is yourself, you are on the road to self-responsibility and empowerment. This is because doing something for yourself is always empowering. If, on the other hand, you have others doing things for you and making your decisions continually, you lose self-esteem and confidence. Therefore don't give away your responsibility by blaming others, whether it be the government, your family, your boss, the customer, or whoever.

I suggest you don't waste time and energy looking for someone to blame when your life doesn't work out the way you wish, but concentrate on looking within to see if you may have caused the situation in some way. Don't take on the guilt, though, as this is also non-productive; it's just blaming another person again – this time yourself. Just because something didn't work out the way you expected doesn't mean that it is wrong. Looking back at the exam example, your failure may be a sign to you that you are on the wrong course. With a positive attitude rather than a guilty or blaming one, you can choose to start something that will be more suitable for you in the long run. Leave out blame entirely, but rather concentrate on how you can change the situation – turn it around and get the best out of it and start planning how to solve it.

So, in summary: concentrate on your own actions rather than those of others; make your own choices; remove the word blame from your vocabulary. This way you can become strong and be empowered.

Self-responsibility at your soul level

I learned through my work as a healer that our higher self can sometimes create situations in our life for its own reason – most often our spiritual development. I obviously wanted to help make the people who came to me feel better, but I soon realised that I wasn't going to be able to heal everyone who I saw. Some people who came to me are sick because they are learning a lesson of their own, a karmic situation that I should not interfere with; some do not want to get better because they are in the state of 'victimhood' and are reluctant to let it go – maybe they enjoy the sympathy they receive. Fortunately, some people are open and ready to heal.

Whatever state my patients are in, whatever their mindset, their higher self has the wisdom to decide if and when they will heal – not me. I pass energy to them, but it is up to them what they do with it. Some people rush home and clean the house from top to bottom with the energies they have received, others will use these energies to improve their health, for example to fight a virus. It is impossible to force wellness upon someone.

Soon after I started healing, I was devastated when a man I had been treating died. He'd had a brain tumour and I'd been determined to cure him. I realised in hindsight that the healing energies had brought him great peace; by the time he died he had accepted his fate and hopefully was happy to move on. It was a lesson for me to let go and to neither anticipate the result of a treatment nor take the responsibility for it on my own shoulders.

It is one of the most exciting and wonderful experiences in the world to offer someone a helping hand and then see them move on to empower themselves, the state that comes from their decision to make their own life choices. We are our own masters, and we dictate and determine our own futures and our own fates. You cannot be responsible for another person. You can love someone and care for them, but you cannot be responsible for them and there is absolutely no point in spending time and energy worrying about someone, no matter how close they are to you. In fact, your negative thoughts or worry and concern will do more harm than good. Think of them as being well and happy. If they are ill, see them free from pain and distress; if they are dying, see them at peace and surrounded by love in the next world.

Be your own master

Self-understanding and healing

When you embark on a spiritual path you need to start by getting to know yourself as well as possible, for how can you heal and improve those aspects of yourself that you haven't acknowledged? You need to face yourself truthfully and discover what makes you tick. You need to accept and evaluate your strengths and weaknesses, and to look deep within yourself to see why you react in certain ways to certain situations and people. You need to go on a journey of self-discovery.

If your car is running slow and obviously has a problem, what do you do? If you don't look under the bonnet, how can you find out what is wrong? If you don't fix the problem, it will get worse. Take time to give yourself a check-up. Be totally honest about your life and your feelings. Is everything fine or have you got old problems still fermenting inside you? Do you still hold resentment towards your parents because of the way they treated you as a child? Do you hold bitterness from past love affairs and relationships? Do you still resent and hate a previous employer because of their unfair treatment of you?

All these issues will cause you emotional pain. If they are not dealt with you will find that the effects of your pent-up emotions will eventually slow you down and cause you mental and then physical problems. They will cripple you spiritually if you do not let them go. This process of finding the hurt – the scars of the past – and reliving and healing them is essential for spiritual growth and inner happiness.

You may have to carry out this inner journey of discovery alongside your normal everyday life, or you may be lucky enough to be able to take yourself away for a time to do so, or you could do a mixture of both. I certainly don't advocate a retreat to the Himalayas, but if that is your wish then good luck; just don't forget to pack the mosquito spray and the Lomatil, and watch out for the altitude!

You don't actually need to go away to search out your scars and the emotions you have bottled up inside you that are affecting your emotional and spiritual health. Every day we are faced with challenges that allow us to discover ourselves. Work situations and our families are particularly good at offering these opportunities. In your journal take notes of everything that you know you have not resolved from your past. Also use it daily as a diary in which you write down everything that has an impact upon you and your reactions. You can, for example, make a note every time you feel these emotions and write down what caused them:

✧ Anger

✧ Frustration

✧ Impatience

✧ Lack of confidence

✧ Fear

✧ Jealousy

Spend time analysing your list and meditate and ponder on your reactions. Don't see yourself as a victim, but realise that any negative reaction is caused by a past experience or an attitude that you hold. Once you have identified the cause of the reaction – your deep-rooted reason – you can start to think about healing it.

✧ Acknowledge that you have an issue or an attitude that needs healing. Claim the problem as your own – don't make the mistake of slipping into 'victimhood' and blaming the person who activated the feelings in you.

✧ Intend that you will solve the problem by healing yourself.

✧ Ask for help from your spirit guides and God if you feel comfortable with this.

✧ Start the healing process – you may need to forgive yourself or someone else, or both; to give yourself more love and respect; to cut your ties to the past or to someone who is causing you pain; to work on your patience or tolerance, and so on.

You can help the self-healing process by bringing in the universal energies of love and compassion. One quick way to do this is to use the symbol below, which I have been given by my spirit guides. The symbol invokes the energies of love and will immediately open a channel to powerful and healing universal energies.

A healing symbol

Draw the symbol in the air three times in the direction indicated, then place your hand on your heart centre, then your solar plexus and finally over your belly button. These are the three main energy centres that suffer from past pain and emotional suffering. The symbol is an intention to bring in the energies of love and light, and they will pass from your hand into your energy and physical body. They will raise the vibrations of your entire energy field and help you release the negative energy that is the root cause of your problem. All negative experiences leave an imprint on our energy fields – the universal energies will help to release this imprint. For more information on self-healing and energy healing you can read my book *Heal Yourself* (*see page 262*).

Patience

This is actually an aspect of unconditional love, but I feel it deserves a place of its own. Patience has been my hardest lesson. I have always been rather impetuous and always want to get things done quickly – to get the idea, seize the moment and do it. This is fine, but it doesn't allow for getting the timing right. The right timing is when all aspects are in place for the greatest good of a situation and the people involved.

As an example, Tony and I decided to sell our house in Buckingham and buy a place that could be our retirement home. We were living in Malaysia at the time so there was no real urgency, but after our house had been on the market for a year I was getting impatient. Eighteen months after it was put up for sale I was visiting the New Forest, where my mother lived, and on the spur of the moment popped into an estate agency to see what properties there were for sale in the area. Tony and I had decided that this would be the preferred location for our retirement. (This was a real act of forward planning as we were in our early fifties at the time.)

A number of houses were available that seemed suitable. I went off to look at the first one on the list but just couldn't find it. I therefore went to see another house in Burley – a small village in the centre of the forest. As I drove up the lane I got very excited. The road was rough and lined with beeches and oaks, and the sun was shining through the leaves; it was quite idyllic and just my idea of a country retreat. I prayed that the house would be suitable. It was absolutely perfect: tucked away from the lane, with a good-sized garden surrounded by trees and paddocks. To put a seal on the entire wonderful experience the owners were absolutely delightful and made me very welcome.

I rang Tony and told him I had found our dream house. There was only one snag – we still hadn't sold our other house. We decided to go ahead anyway and buy this one, and started to talk bridging loans and tenancy – not the ideal situation, but we just couldn't let this house go. Then divine timing showed its hand. The very next week our house in Buckingham was sold!

Trust and surrender to divine timing

Sometimes delays are created quite deliberately by divine interference; by intervention from our guides and angels. They can see the bigger picture and for our greatest good will often delay matters. This is why patience is called a virtue. It is really a form of faith – faith that things will be as they are meant to be and that the outcomes for our plans will be as they should be.

There is another aspect to patience and that is having patience with other people. This aligns with tolerance and is a matter of teaching yourself discipline and control – to hold back from being hasty with criticism or acting in a short and aggressive manner with someone who seems slow.

Be patient with yourself, with others and with life in general – it is a great discipline and it aligns you with the state of love. Remember that you are not a saint, though. If you catch yourself getting irritated by someone don't place yourself in a state of guilt – it will not help you or them. Just try a bit harder the next time.

A positive attitude

From a healer's perspective I know that taking a positive attitude to life can make the difference to a person's well-being and health. Because our thoughts are energy any negative thoughts we have, particularly about ourselves, will lodge in the energy field that surrounds our physical body – our aura. Over time the energy of consistent negative thoughts, like worries or anxieties, congeal and create blocks in our energy. After a while these inhibit the natural flow of our body's energy and we become ill.

In order for you to have a healthy body and mind, it is essential that you keep yourself as positive as possible. From a spiritual point of view it is impossible to be happy when you are harbouring negative thoughts, such as jealousy, dislike, hatred, irritation, impatience, distrust, and so on.

As your objective is to be happy you need to work on your attitude and presence as a priority. Look for the good in every situation and the benefits that you will gain from every experience. Every single thing that happens to you is helping you towards your goal, so see the events of your life in a positive way – see that they are gifts towards your evolvement and eventual inner happiness and peace. Remember that any downturns and suffering you experience will help you to gain wisdom and compassion for the suffering and problems of others. It will make you a better person.

A powerful way of uplifting yourself and others is through a sense of humour. I've heard it said that God must have an incredible sense of humour to have created camels and sex. A good sense of humour will carry you through many of the ups and downs of life, and will allow you to bring things into perspective when they get out of proportion. Laughing at yourself can be a huge ice-breaker and a diffuser of awkward atmospheres, and it creates great bridges between people of all backgrounds.

I have two friends, Angie and Pam, who are particularly good at seeing the funny side of even the most dramatic and disastrous events in their lives. Whenever I have a call from either of them we end up laughing hysterically and it's often at their expense. It is a habit they have developed for coping with things that go wrong, but it has a great effect for them and for their friends.

My mother is also full of stories about the ridiculous things she has done, like putting the hot-water bottle in the fridge and leaving the kettle outside for the milkman – as she gets slightly more absent-minded so the stories get funnier. I'd better say right here and now that she is not slipping into senility – it's just that her short-term memory is not what it was. Instead of worrying about this she just uses it as an excuse for a laugh. Look for the ridiculous in situations, particularly when they are tense and becoming dramatic; search for the funny side in everything. You will enjoy life a great deal more, and you will have more to share at a social event than would otherwise be the case. Fun is a perspective – a way of looking at life.

> There is fun in everything –
> it just needs to be uncovered

Confidence

I see confidence as a lack of fear, and as fear is the greatest obstacle in your spiritual path it is the one I suggest you focus on and work on as much as you can. The feeling of being out of control, or worse still in the control of some outside force or fear, is the worst state to be in. My suggestion for an effective way to clear away fears is firstly to get an understanding of their cause and then to face them. This is the only way I have managed to overcome my personal fears. I have attempted to do all the things that have frightened me the most, whether it be going into tunnels and caves, speaking in front of large audiences, or being near horses. Overcoming a fear is the most revitalising and uplifting thing you can do – I promise you. It does wonders for your self-esteem and confidence.

Your fears are your greatest enemies. They will take away the light in your life. They can stop your progress, make you act aggressively towards those you love, disturb your days and give you nightmares through the long hours of darkness. Make being without fear one of your greatest aspirations. I am not talking about the fear of loud noises, other people's aggression or danger – these are natural and life-saving fears that will spur you to action to protect yourself. I am talking about needless fear resulting from your past experiences or generated by other people. If a fear is caused by your past you need to work through the situation. With the help of counsellors, therapists and healers, intend to move beyond it and leave the cause behind you, otherwise your life will be limited in terms of happiness and contentment.

You cannot have true peace if you are vulnerable to attacks of mindless fear. We are bombarded by the words and stimulation of fearmongers every day of our lives; stories and impressions are pasted on to our sensitive minds and emotions by those who make a living out of stirring up our negativity. Most newspapers thrive on creating fear. Sensational stories and articles on health hazards have been very popular in the last 20 years. As I am writing this book in Hong Kong, we are being paralysed by the fear of Severe Acute Respiratory Syndrome (SARS). The disease has caught the imagination of the press, and the fear induced by stories about it has bankrupted thousands of businesses as people stay away from the island.

I sometimes think that the fear is more contagious than the disease. In the past we were fed a fear of the demons of the East or West, depending on where we lived. The Cold War was a creation of fear by political leaders that was fuelled by the media. Political despots use fear to control their people. Fear controls and is therefore a great tool for those who want to control us in any way. I have just been observing the downfall of Saddam Hussein, who has held his country, Iraq, in the grip of fear for 30 years. It is quite amazing to see people who have lived in terror for their entire lives suddenly become free.

Fear is therefore the tool that is used to control people, whether it be at a national level, or in the workplace or home. You have to manage your own emotions and intend that you will not be hoodwinked and deceived – that you will be able to see the truth behind the deceptions and make up your own mind. At a personal level, avoid creating your own demons. Face them and see them for what they really are. You will need to work with honesty and clarity to pinpoint the cause of your fear. Remember that most fears will dissipate when confronted and then you can step along your path with confidence.

Fear creates hurdles on our path

Self-esteem

This aspiration did not appear in ancient spiritual creeds. In the past spiritual teachers were more concerned with you keeping your ego in check and being humble. However, if you have low self-esteem, you will be living your life at half-pace. This is akin to living in fear and it restricts and disables you. It stops you being as big as you can be, and limits the contribution you can make to the world.

The basis of most low self-esteem is lack of self-respect and self-love. This may have been caused by the attitudes of those around you as you were developing and growing, especially in your childhood. Improving your self-esteem is, however, an important aspiration to aim for. You need to respect yourself and care for yourself, for only once you treat yourself well can you love and care for those around you. This subject is covered in greater detail in Chapter 7.

Chapter Five

ACCESSING UNIVERSAL AND PERSONAL POWERS

During your life there may be times when you feel that you would appreciate some help in achieving your personal goals and ambitions. There will be times when you feel helpless – when life is particularly difficult and challenging. There may be times when you would really like to make a contribution to changing not only your life but also the lives of those you love. You may also want to help bring peace and love to the world. In the past we have been encouraged to pray for this help – to ask our God to help us reach our goals and change our circumstances.

In the twenty-first century I think it is appropriate for us to look for our own ability to reach our goals and to change our circumstances by accessing our personal and universal energies, which will give us the power to enable these changes. I still believe in prayer, however, and you will see that it is one of the powers I suggest you use. Other powers are personal and are there within you waiting to be accessed and utilised to their fullest extent.

The powers of the universe are available to all of us. Some of them have been hidden from us; others have been known to us but we have not utilised them to their greatest effect. Used properly and with good intention, they can transform your life and smooth your path in the most remarkable way. They are the antidote to many of life's frustrations and will help you over many of the hurdles and challenges that you face in your day-to-day existence. I believe in all the powers that I introduce to you here. They have all been instrumental in the transformation of my own life, and although they are incredibly powerful they are simple to use. You will need to keep focused and be patient, for sometimes it will take time for them to come into full action. You must also always work with the very best of intentions for all.

The powers that you can use are:

- The power of intention

- The power of will, or free choice

- The power of visualisation

- The power of prayer

- The power of detachment

- The power of attraction

- Healing powers:
    - The power of light
    - The power of love

POWERS FOR CREATING AND MANIFESTING YOUR NEEDS

You have at your disposal, for use in your daily life, incredible sources of personal power that many of us either misuse or use too sparingly – the powers of intention and will. These are associated with the aspect of your mind that allows you to make your own choices, to create the life that you want.

I have great faith in the power of the human mind. I believe the mind is integrated with our entire character, personality, genetic inheritance and, importantly, our soul. It is not a blob in the middle of our head, lost in our brain. The brain is a mechanism that is a transmitter and receiver (and a lot else medically), and it is a physical part of our being. The mind, however, is governed by our spirit. We can therefore use it to determine and direct our lives and the things that happen to us.

The four powers described here are used for manifesting – for bringing your ideas, thoughts and hopes into reality and creating the things you need in your life. They can be used, for instance, to help you to find a home or a job. They can also assist you in reaching a personal goal such as starting your own company, losing weight or helping others. As an example, if I plan a seminar I use these powers to help me find a suitable venue and bring in the requisite number of people. The four powers are:

✧ Intention – what we choose

✧ Will – the force of our spirit to activate our intention

✧ Visualisation – the image of our goal, the blueprint of our expec-
   tation

✧ Prayer – the inclusion of divine help and the surrender to the
   universe for the method of the manifestation

The power of intention

Our intention is a powerful tool for action and for creating what we want. When we continuously intend a particular thing to happen and use the power of our will – it must happen. This is a natural law and cannot be broken. We can, however, confuse the energies of this law by changing our minds, being fluffy about our choices, or intending one thing and then acting contrarily. It is therefore important for you to remember when you use the powers of manifesting that you must keep your intentions consistent. If you intend to lose weight, don't stock your cupboards with chocolates and sweets. If you intend to change jobs, don't refuse to talk to the personnel officer. For manifestation to take place your will needs to work with your intentions.

The power of will, or free choice

Will power is the force that we need to put behind our intentions. It is our spirit – our part of the spirit of all – that we can connect to our choice. We are gifted with will power and it enables us to make choices and therefore to create. It is essential that our spirit keeps us going when we have a setback; it is our spirit – our will – that must endure. If our spirit falters; if we give up as soon as the going gets tough; if our will power dissolves in adversity, then we will never create our dreams.

Humanity is blessed with an amazing capacity for will, as we have seen over the centuries. Just think of some of the terrible atrocities and persecutions that have challenged communities, cultures and races – yet they have generally endured to rise up again. Think of how despots such as Stalin, Hitler and Pol Pot have decimated their people – how they tried to crush the spirit of their people but couldn't. In my opinion you would have to kill every man, woman and child on Earth to crush humanity. We just need to tap into that great spirit that is within each of us to create our dreams.

We can use our will to make our choices, to say no to that which we know is wrong – maybe we should be more active in doing this. In politics we have the opportunity to vote for the people who we want as our countries leaders, but how many of us actually take advantage of that vote? We can petition and lobby for the downtrodden and the disadvantaged in our own country and overseas – but do we use this power?

Let's look at the great gift of free choice – the law that allows us to make our own decisions on Earth. We may take this for granted, but it is amazing that despite the fact that God has immense power, intelligence and understanding, he does not interfere with the way that we run our lives. We live by the laws of the universe in that karma automatically brings back misfortune to us if we hurt others, but God doesn't arbitrarily give us a smack on the ear when we do something wrong. The ebb and flow of energy and the cycles and rhythms of the world he has created perform the monitoring that we need. For example, if we work too hard we get exhausted; if we drink too much alcohol we poison our bodies and get physically ill; if we consistently think negatively we become depressed and mentally sick, and so on.

We have the freedom to choose what we eat, think and do. We can therefore determine to a great extent what happens to us. We are, of course, influenced by the choices that we made before we were born, when we laid down the blueprint of our life. But we can make changes to this: as we go along we can tweak the script as it suits us. We therefore really do get the best of both worlds – what we chose in the spirit world and what we now choose in our reality.

I often feel that we under-utilise this great gift. We allow ourselves to be influenced and dominated by the dictates of others. In my lifetime I have seen entire nations ruled and dominated by the persuasion and inclinations of one man. We allow ourselves to be limited in our horizons by the limitations of our parents, our culture and our country.

One example that comes into my mind concerns the desire for peace. Most people, if you ask them, want peace. They just want the chance to get along with their lives and leave others to live theirs. Why therefore do we allow ourselves to be dragged into conflict and war? We can choose: let's do so. We can use our freedom of choice once we leave our parental care – if we use it wisely we can create fulfilling and meaningful lives for ourselves;

lives without limitations where we aim for the best and achieve the best.

When you make your choices try always to consult your feelings, rather than be ruled by logic. The best decisions and the most spiritually aware choices are those that come from the heart rather than the head. Say out loud what you are planning to do, discuss it with friends and take note of your own senses as you speak. Do you feel good inside or do you feel unsure? Do the words ring true and clear, or are you muddled and confused as you speak? Do you feel strong or weak as you verbalise your plans? As a general rule do things that you want to do – bearing in mind you must harm no one with your choice – rather than things that please others.

You can use the power of your will in your daily life at a more mundane level. For example, if you wish to give up smoking – which my husband has just done – make it your intention to do so. If you put your will – your spirit – behind this intention and are single-minded, you will give up smoking, as my husband has. If you believe you can do it, you will do it. If, however, you doubt yourself, you take away your own power with your lack of faith and are likely to fail. When you have doubts you are not fully intending to carry through your intention – you are saying that you can give up, as long as you are strong enough. The other reason why you may fail is that you change your mind and say to yourself that you like smoking and want to carry on. In this case you are intending to carry on with your desire and want.

Your intention plus your will always form the driving force to create the outcome. Whatever you intend will happen. You can manifest anything you wish. Try it for yourself. Be single-minded and watch out for self-doubt, because that removes the will and changes the intention. Also check that what you desire and intend to create is what you really want and will be beneficial to you!

Positive declarations – giving power to your intentions

A useful way of focusing your intention on changes that you want to make in yourself is to use positive declarations. These are statements; affirmations of how you want to be. There are a few rules:

✧ Use the present tense, for example 'I am', rather than 'I will be'.

✧ Use only positive expressions, for example 'I do', rather than 'I do not'.

✧ Repeat your declarations out loud as often as you can.

> Freedom of choice is your greatest gift – use it

The power of visualisation

This is the last in the series of manifestations that *create*. When the world was evolved and created by the word of God he used these powers. He intended to create, visualised what it was that he wanted, and then used his will, *the will of God*, to turn it into reality. We are made of the same 'stuff' as God, and therefore we can also create.

Visualisation is a powerful tool. It creates a blueprint of what you plan to make – to create. Whenever I have a plan I write it down – this is the intention and the start of the blueprint. I mull over the plan for a while and ask for help. I meditate and pray, and gradually get a firmer and firmer idea of my goal. I then start to visualise the dream or plan as if it exists already. Very often I don't get too particular about detail. For example, if you want a cottage in the country envisage and sense peace, calm, the countryside, beauty and a pretty garden, and leave it at that.

Don't go into great detail because this way you could enforce what may not be the perfect home for you. I let God and the universe work on the best detail.

How do you use visualisation? Think of what you want: if it is, say, a state of being, then imagine yourself in that state. Now hold the picture of it in your mind. If you have difficulty imagining the picture use symbols. Alternatively, it may help you to draw a picture of what you want and hold that picture in your mind. Here are some examples of the sorts of associations that you can use:

✧ Academic success: a graduation mortarboard or a certificate

✧ Happiness: a smiley face

✧ Peace: a white dove

✧ Prosperity: bundles of money or piles of coins

✧ Love: a heart or cupid

✧ Success: champagne bottles popping, or other symbols of celebration

To place a vision in a specific time frame you can make a clock with the time and date part of your visualisation.

If you want to be clear of a negative characteristic, for example if you are struggling with anger, see yourself at peace – see doves flying around you. Always see the opposite state to the one you are trying to rid yourself of – for impatience see calm (for instance waves lapping gently on a beach), for weakness and indecision see a strong muscular arm and other symbols of strength, and so on.

If you find it completely impossible to visualise, put your drawing on the refrigerator door and make a point of looking at it every day to remind yourself of your goal.

The power of prayer

I have already spent some time on the power of prayer (*see page 52*) but I want to mention it again here as it is one of the great spiritual powers. It is also the final power I use when manifesting. I pass my visualisation of my dream or plan to God – I surrender to the universe with the words, 'If this for the highest good of all let it manifest.' This allows for a higher and larger plan that may or may not include my 'dream'.

To summarise how to use the great spiritual power of manifestation:

❖ INVOKE THE POWER OF INTENTION – Think of what you want, then intend that you will achieve it.

❖ INVOKE THE POWER OF WILL – Connect to your spirit by determination and commitment to your intention.

❖ INVOKE THE POWER OF VISUALISATION – Draw, write and imagine your dream in action; visualise it as a reality and in the present.

❖ INVOKE THE POWER OF PRAYER – Surrender your plan to God and the universe, and ask that it be manifested if it is for the highest good of all.

The power of detachment

One of the great sources of pain and upset is attachment to material possessions and people. Caring and feeling for people, homes and cherished objects is not a problem. It is your attitude towards possession that can give you trouble. When you consider that you own something or somebody you create a vulnerability for yourself because it is impossible to ensure complete ownership of anything. A possession may be stolen, lost or destroyed; you can never be totally in control of it no matter how hard you try – and, after all, once you move on from this life all those possessions will be left behind, so they cannot be bonded to you for ever.

How do we get attached?

As mentioned earlier (*see page 96*), every thought that we have is energy. If we continually think of someone with love, the energy between us is so constant that it becomes an etheric cord which links us together. Such cords are referred to as heart strings in our love songs and poetry. Being attached to someone is therefore just that – it means that we are linked by these etheric or energy cords.

Attachments of love

When two people love each other, whether they be brother and sister, two friends, lovers, or parent and child, two intertwined cords (one from each of them) will link them together. These two cords will stay in place as long as the thoughts of love are constant. If one person moves away, falls out of love or dies, their cord is broken and the other person will feel the pain of the dislocation. The pain is real and is felt in the heart centre, the energy centre of your body that sits in the middle of the chest. Have you ever felt the pain of loss? If you have, you will know how real the pain is.

The linking energy strings will be created whenever you let your emotions centre extensively on one person or one particular place or object. You become attached if you focus on one thing and your emotions are involved. When the object of your desire is removed you feel pain. Sai Baba, one of the great spiritual teachers of India, teaches that all pain is caused by attachment. I can understand this, because we always feel pain if we lose something or someone to whom we are attached.

The attachment to possessions

It is one thing to be attached to a person through love, but when we attach ourselves to material things we are really creating problems for ourselves. I am encouraging you to move to a state of harmony and peace. If you become attached to material possessions, whether they be your jewellery, your home or gifts you have received, you will be vulnerable and will have the potential to be badly hurt. At this point you may say that it is surely OK to love the gifts you've been given, particularly the ones that have some sentimental value to you. Well, I can tell you how I handle this. At the time when I receive a gift, I see it as a visible manifestation of someone's love. The love is gratefully received – at the time when the gift is given I take the love and appreciate it. The energy exchange therefore consists of the thought of the person presenting the gift and the thanks and appreciation shown in return. The gift has now done its job.

Try to look at your material possessions as gifts that are loaned to you for a time. Enjoy them and be thankful for them, and when the time is right let them go. If you become too attached to them you will end up being the possessed – you will come to rely on them for your happiness and will be distraught if you lose them. Should your possessions be lost, stolen or sold, trust that they are where they should be. Perhaps they are helping someone else; maybe they are lightening the life of another person who has a greater need for them than you do. This is the power of detachment – the ability to let go – in action.

Your home

What about your home? To my mind a home is about memories – the good times you have had in it. I had a flat in Dunstable, where I lived as a single woman before I left for South Africa. I lived there for a couple of years and as I was working for a lively young company I spent most of my time out and about with my work colleagues or friends. I did little entertaining in the flat and rarely shared it with anyone. It was therefore very easy to sell it when I wanted to move on. I had little sentimental attachment to it.

My current home in Burley is the opposite of the flat. It is the place where the entire family meets and we have had many wonderful times there. When I die it will not go with me – but the memory of it can. Nothing will take away the memories of the house, the garden, the love shared and the happy times. I don't support the belief that we should be completely detached from our homes, and to a certain extent our possessions, as through our cords of attachment we actually receive love. When I think of my garden at home and the great beech tree that dominates it, I actually feel love in my heart, so there is a two-way flow of love even from inanimate objects.

Your expectations

Another instance when we can be hurt is when our expectations are not met. We are potentially vulnerable if we are attached to outcomes. In the process of manifesting described above the last stage was surrender. This surrender is in fact a form of detachment: it is a passing of your dreams and needs to the universe; a surrender to the greater consciousness. This may be somewhat problematic for control freaks or even those of us (and I include myself here) who like to see things through to the end and want to take full responsibility for all projects, plans, and so on. However, if we put our best efforts into action – if we do all that we possibly can to ensure the success of our plans and follow the manifesting process – then what else is there for us to do?

What we usually do is sit and worry about the result of our efforts. We become impatient about things like timing and anxious if our expected results do not materialise. *Don't do this!* Once you have done all you can, surrender the outcome. Become detached from the outcome and your expectations. I have tried this and I can tell you that it works very well. If the result is as you wished it to be you are delighted, and if it is not you know that it was not meant to be and you have not spent all your energy in fretting and worrying. You can then see what else you can do that may be nearer the mark, or wait for the right timing.

The power of detachment comes fully into operation when

you let go of those things that no longer serve you or bring you happiness and joy. For example, if your partner leaves you cut the cords and let them go. You are no longer receiving love so your attachment is a drain on your energy and your love. If you have moved from a house or country permanently, let it go – cut the cords. Keep the good memories in your heart but no longer yearn for what is in the past.

> Enjoy your possessions but don't be
> possessed by them – be free

The power of attraction

There is a strange phenomenon that occurs when you start to see life from a new perspective. Once you start to follow a spiritual path intentionally you will find that you suddenly seem to meet other people with a similar interest. When I began my healing work I found that I met a number of people who were also healers or were interested in alternative healing therapies or spiritual matters. They seemed to come out of the woodwork! Wherever I went I seemed to be bumping into them. Let me give you an example of how this happened.

While I was lived in Kuala Lumpur I took a short holiday with a couple of girlfriends on the east coast island of Berhentian. We asked the local boatman if he knew of a quiet place he could take us to, where we could meditate and I could do some healing for my friends. He said he knew just the place – a small island nearby that was completely deserted. He dropped us off at this idyllic place and we spent some time enjoying the absolute peace.

Some time later I was healing one of my friends when another boat turned up and two women got out and started walking up the beach, chatting and laughing. My other friend approached them and asked them if they wouldn't mind being quiet just for a while until I finished the healing session. They agreed.

When I had finished one of the women approached me and asked about the healing, saying that she too was a healer. She was visiting Malaysia on business and had taken a few days' holiday, having just finished her work teaching marketing at one of the business colleges. We immediately established a wonderful rapport and became friends in no time. In fact, she joined me a month later and helped me with a healing workshop. She specialised in sound healing and I had a session in my workshop dedicated to that subject. The strange thing was that on the day I was supposed to cover the sound session I became ill and my new-found friend stepped in. This was the first time she had taught and it was a step she needed to take – so we both benefited greatly from our meeting.

This was the power of attraction in action. We attract people with a similar energy to ours – people who are on the same wavelength as us. As we are beings of energy, so we send out a certain wavelength. The level of energy we send out depends on our state of mind, our intentions and our emotions. If we are happy we send out light energy, high vibrations. If we are sad, depressed, angry or filled with hate we send out varying degrees of low-vibration energy. Light and positive thoughts create light energy, dark and negative thoughts create heavy energy.

You may well know this from your relationships with the people you meet in your everyday life. When you are with someone who is sunny and upbeat, you can feel their mood affecting you too. You will therefore find that if you are predominantly a positive person with a bright outlook on life you will attract people with similar attitudes. You will consciously and unconsciously reject those whose energy does not match yours.

This is, of course, very important when choosing a partner. You would not want to spend a great deal of your time with someone whose energy is totally different from yours. Of course, we change as we go through life and this is one of the reasons why so many marriages do not last – because as we change we pull different people towards us. I discuss relationships a great deal more later, but this is one factor that you need to be aware of when you make a decision to choose a partner. Are you drawn together naturally and do you feel comfortable in each other's presence, or are you choosing your partner for other reasons?

You may find that when you embark on your spiritual path you will lose some of your friends – this is the natural attraction/rejection process in action. Be philosophical about it. Don't cling to the past – although I know you will want to be loyal to old friends. I have found that those friends who think like I do are still in my life – some more often than others, but the closeness we have has survived my 'new ways' – while those who reject my beliefs have faded into the background. One day you may meet up again with such friends and find that the attraction is there again. In the meantime just let it be; you cannot force friendship.

Loving people attract loving people

Healing powers

As we are beings of energy, so our thoughts are energy and the emotions attached to them are transmitted to the subject of their focus. This means that when we think of someone with love they will be affected by that love. The scientific law of energy is that it cannot go away, disappear or be dissolved, although it can change its form. So, when we think of someone with love they will be affected by the vibration of the energy we are sending – love is the highest vibration of energy. When they receive this high-vibration energy they can use it to lift their spirits, to heal an illness or to give them the zest to spring-clean the kitchen.

The same principle applies to negative energy. If you have dark and negative thoughts about yourself and your future, the energy will cling to you and bring you down in every way. Negative thoughts sent to another will also have these effects.

You can use this law to its greatest advantage by sending distant healing to those who you know need to be lifted, and to lift your own energies by clearing your own mind of anxieties and worries. Personally, I find the easiest way to stop myself from worrying is to deliberately send streams of light and love to someone I know. This technique will allow you to take your mind off your own woes while at the same time benefiting someone else.

Activating and spreading the power of love and light

To my mind consciously activating and spreading light is one of the most beneficial things we can do. By light I mean divine light – some call it the light of Christ's consciousness, which is the energy and life essence that Jesus brought to Earth in the form of the message to love all, to forgive your enemies and to show the kindly and caring face of God. Once the world is filled with this light, fear, prejudice, emotional suffering, wars – in fact all forms of evil and darkness – will be at an end. This light is the cosmic light of universal love; it is unconditional love.

You can bring light into the lives of the people who surround you at home, at work and at play; and you can do this either subconsciously or consciously. Let's first look at how you can lighten the world with your presence, your attitude and your thoughts. You can bring light into the world by the way you are – by the way you think and feel, by the way you treat yourself and others. Positive attitudes and positive actions bring in the light of love.

Shedding light around you by just being yourself

Every time you smile or laugh, every time you think lovingly or kindly of someone or something, you are bringing in the cosmic light of love. Caring thoughts are the energy thoughts of love, and they will affect whatever is in their attention. The energy of a thought goes as a stream of high-vibration energy directly to the point of its focus. So a positive attitude actually brings light into the world.

Some people unconsciously dedicate their lives to bringing in light. Many entertainers, comedians, actors, musicians and singers spread light with their work. Writers, scriptwriters and poets who give us insights, uplift us, encourage us, make us feel good or make us laugh are helping to bring in positive vibrations to the world. Artists of all mediums spread light with their creations. Film-makers lift our spirits with their creative art on celluloid. All acts of creation that are designed to lift the spirit, make us laugh, and show us passion and compassion are subconsciously light bearers. Doctors, nurses and therapists, those working with animals and the environment, and those helping to improve the social and physical well-being of people around the world are helping with the enlightenment of all of humanity.

Even if you are not dedicating your life to any of this work you can and do bring light with your actions, thoughts and deeds. When you help someone feel better emotionally, physically or spiritually – all these are linked – you are lighting up their lives. Every positive thought counts in this aspiration. When you smile at the check-out girl and ask how she is, when you thank the doorman, the postman or the office cleaner and acknowledge their efforts, when you ring a friend to cheer them up, send a card, give a gift, listen to someone's problems, let a car in ahead of you in the traffic, you are bringing in light. Just by being happy and content within yourself – just by being you – you become a messenger of light.

As you work your way along your spiritual path, clearing away old thought processes, releasing limitations put upon you by others or by your experiences, as you develop your self-healing skills and learn to accept yourself totally and unconditionally, so your ability to bring light to yourself and those around you will improve. People will start to say that you look so much lighter, and ask what you have done to yourself. It will just be the manifestation of the love within you growing. You will truly be activating the ripple effect.

I have a great faith in the future of humanity and our world, and I believe in the strength of the human spirit: in our determination to overcome our problems; in the total commitment of mankind to survive; in the desire of the people of the world to live in a peaceful and harmonious state with each other and the environment. However, we have to face the fact that the world is in a rather desperate state at the moment.

The environment and whole food chain are polluted and toxic; there is a shortage of good water; the land has been eroded through bad farming practices; the rainforests have been depleted, and there are many other environmental problems. Is there anything you can do to help apart from having a personal commitment to relieve these situations where you can on a practical level? Is there anything you can do on a daily basis? The answer is yes, there is.

Consciously bringing in light

This is a subject for which I have great passion. I truly believe that at this time it is imperative that we consciously assist in changing the energies of the world. I work with energy streams as a norm and so tend to see most situations in terms of energy. The conflicts, the power struggles and the greed of people, communities and nations are the results of the creation of more negativity and darkness. The main cause of darkness on Earth is fear. As the leaders of nations postulate war they instil and build fear in people.

If we look back over the last century, individuals have been the cause of immense darkness – tremendous fear. Let's take Stalin as an example. Through his regime of terror he dominated the people of the Soviet Union by creating fear. This fear has left most people now, although all those in the older generations who were once fearful of the heavy footsteps of the KGB leading to their door will be scarred by the experience. They will find it hard to relax and be totally at peace within themselves because the old fear will still lurk there – to be woken by sounds in the night or dreams and nightmares of the past.

There are still tyrants with the same agenda running countries and communities all over the world today – from Zimbabwe to housing estates in London. Gangs of young men who terrorise the people in their communities, thugs who run prostitution and drug empires, and dictators who overwhelm their countries with their desire for money and power all create darkness; all create vast streams of negative energy that need to be cleared. Moreover every individual act of hatred and vengeance, no matter how small, every spiteful comment, every hurtful act or word creates negative energy. Let's see what can be done to offset and transform this negativity.

I am going to cover two ways in which we can bring in light (although there are many, of course):

✧ Distance, or absent, healing, which is the intention to send energy streams of light and love to a given place, situation or person.

✧ The creation of healing from within, which is being and feeling the state that you wish to create for yourself or others.

DISTANCE HEALING

To send healing you only need the intention, enough love and caring to do it, and a few moments of your time. What you will be doing is not necessarily healing, but sending the energy to someone to enable them to perform their own healing if that is their wish. You cannot force anyone to do anything they do not wish to do. It is for the soul and higher essence of a person – their subconscious, if you like – to decide what they will do with the energy that you send them. This is an important fact to remember: dominating or controlling anyone with our thoughts is not the intention – there was enough of that practised in the Cold War era.

When you think of someone and intend to help them you set off a reaction. Your thoughts transport the emotions or feelings that you are holding. If you are thinking of love and the well-being of the person, they will receive these high vibrations of energy – the energy goes to the focus of your attention.

MEDITATION FOR SENDING THE ENERGIES OF LOVE

❖ Find a quiet place on the ground, turn off the phones, light a candle and relax. You can burn aromatherapy oils if you wish to help in your relaxation. Lavender, for instance, is great for calming you down.

❖ Close your eyes, drop your shoulders and let your body go limp.

❖ Breathe deeply four or five times; breathe in deeply and slowly.

❖ Ask for spiritual help if you wish, from God or angels, or any spiritual connection that feels right for you.

❖ Connect to the ground on which you are sitting or lying. See roots growing from the bottom of your feet deep down into the earth beneath.

❖ See the roots reaching down through many strata of the Earth's crust.

❖ See them growing through underground streams and deeper and deeper into the very centre of the Earth.

❖ Imagine a large, clear quartz crystal in the centre and see your roots connecting to this.

✧ Allow yourself to open to the nourishing and loving energies of Mother Earth.

✧ Sense that love rising up through your roots in the form of light – loving, healing light.

✧ Sense the light energy coming into your body and moving to your heart centre.

✧ Sense the light filling your heart with loving energy and clearing away all negativity in your being.

✧ Concentrate on your heart and feel love for all humanity, all that lives on Earth and in the rest of the universe.

✧ See beams of loving energy leaving your heart as streams of light and reaching out to the person or situation you are helping.

✧ Say, 'Take this loving energy and use it as you will – for your highest good.'

✧ See the person totally immersed and surrounded by your love. See them as though they are lit up by a thousand floodlights. Just do this for a few minutes for all those you wish to help.

✧ Finally place your hands on your heart and let the love now move through your own body, healing and revitalising you.

MEDITATION FOR CHANNELLING LIGHT AND SENDING IT ON

In this process you act as a conduit for divine energies. You become a bridge between the cosmic source of light and the person or situation that you wish to assist. You will be connecting directly to a source of the highest vibration of energy in the universe.

✧ Find a quiet place, preferably away from other people, turn off the phones and shut the door.

✧ Breathe in deeply several times, letting out all your negative thoughts and anxieties as you breathe out and breathing in a stream of clear, light air.

✧ Call in your angels and spirit guides.

✧ Imagine that you are surrounded by purple flames – this is a good, strong protection that you will need because you are opening up to the spirit world, and not every spirit being is from the light.

✧ See roots growing from your feet down into the earth beneath you. See them reach the centre of the Earth and connect to a clear quartz crystal that symbolises the heart and soul of Mother Earth.

✧ Let the earthly energies of love and light move up through your feet and legs until your entire being is filled with the nurturing Earth energies of nature.

✧ Connect to your spiritual strength by saying, 'I connect to the highest energies of love and compassion.' If you wish you can connect directly to God, to Jesus or to any other spiritual leader or Master that you favour.

✧ Visualise the divine energies of cosmic love and light coming down from the skies through your crown chakra (see page 16).

✧ Now you are filled with these wonderful energies. Think of the person or situation that you want to help and say, 'I send you the highest energies of love and compassion; do with them as you will.' See beams of light reaching out from you, your heart centre and your hands towards the person you are helping.

✧ If this is a global healing visualise the planet between your hands and know that the energies are filling the world and bringing light to all that need it.

MEDITATION FOR VISUALISING A PERSON WELL

In this meditation you are using the power of your imagination to visualise the situation that you want to create. This is an act of manifestation created by your will, your intention and your love.

✧ Find a quiet place to relax and unwind.

✧ Breathe deeply to bring your body into a state of calm.

✧ Drop your shoulders and let your body become soft and pliant.

✧ Let your feet be heavy and allow yourself to meld to the floor and the ground beneath you.

✧ Call upon any spiritual assistance that you may wish for.

✧ Bring the person or situation who you wish to help into your mind. If you have a photograph, hold it in your hands to help make the connection to their energies. Ask that you may be guided for the highest good of all concerned.

✧ If it is a person you are helping see them well and happy. If they are sick see them recovered and in good health. If they are depressed see them in good spirits. Use your imagination and your knowledge of them to place them in the best possible state.

✧ If it is a conflict or natural disaster you are helping, see the people and nations concerned at peace with one another, or the landscape flourishing and recovered from the disaster.

✧ You can use symbols to help with your visualisation. If you want a venture or project to be successful, see people raising champagne glasses, or cheering and applauding.

✧ See the person, group or situation filled with light.

THE CREATION OF HEALING FROM WITHIN
This is how the ripple effect works – if we create peace within ourselves, those around us will also be affected. Let's just look

again at the principle that every living thing is connected spiritually and energetically and see how we can make use of this to help the world.

Every single living thing comes from the same source – the consciousness of God, the creator of all, the highest form of love and light – and therefore every living thing is connected through the energy of this consciousness. It is rather as if you had a piece of modelling dough and moulded a number of little people out of it. The common denominator would be the modelling dough, and whatever vibration was in the original piece of dough would be in the individual pieces created from it. They would also be of the same colour and density.

Our connection to each other provides us with empathy, and in some cases we actually share our emotional and even physical experiences with others. If you are a dog owner you may have experienced the sixth sense that allows your dog to pick up what is happening to other dogs in your area. One night a couple of years ago both my dogs cried and howled for no apparent reason. This went on for quite some time and it wasn't until the following morning that I learned that a dog had been killed in the street near our home. We are linked to all that is living – and that includes the animal kingdom, the vegetable kingdom and the mineral kingdom.

We can use this connection between us all to assist the state of the entire human race. By putting yourself into the state of peace you can begin the change that will make everyone feel peace.

MEDITATION TO BE IN THE STATE OF PEACE

Returning to the process of healing using this principle, by being in the state that you wish for others you will pass that state to them. You can use this process to bring peace to the world.

✧ Make yourself comfortable in a quiet and restful environment. If you wish play some peaceful and calming music.

✧ Close your eyes and relax.

✧ Breathe in deeply four or five times until your heartbeat has slowed and your body is calm.

✧ Imagine you are a tree with your roots growing into the earth beneath you – if you cannot see this in your imagination, just know that you are truly connected to the Earth.

✧ Take a few moments to consider the source of your creation. If you wish you can speak to God, or to your perception of creation at this time. Acknowledge the love that initiated the creation of all.

✧ Now sense peace in your heart centre (the energy centre in the middle of your chest). See swirls of pink light creating a vortex in this centre. Concentrate on the feelings of love and peace.

✧ You can use your imagination in any way you wish to achieve the feeling of peace. Choose a way that will work for you, for example:

  ✦ Think of someone you love.

  ✦ Think of a beautiful scene in nature like a setting sun over a calm lake, a serene beach scene, a forest, or whatever else is appropriate for you.

  ✦ Visualise a white dove – a universal symbol of peace.

  ✦ See children of different races holding hands or playing together in harmony.

  ✦ See people of many nations gathering together to help each other on some project like building a sanctuary or helping the aged or ill.

  ✦ Focus on someone who represents feelings of love and peace – perhaps a public figure who has dedicated their life to these ends.

✧ Once you have achieved these feelings within you intend that they migrate to the entire world.

✧ Sit and enjoy this wonderful state for as long as you wish.

You now have most of the information you need for changing your way of being, for starting your transformation. You have a philosophy that you can work with, the knowledge of spiritual beings that can help, and the personal and universal powers to enable you to create. Before we look at ways in which you can integrate this philosophy into everyday-life situations, let's go through some of the outcomes you can expect to come out of these changes.

Chapter Six

YOUR JOURNEY SO FAR

This chapter looks at the results that you can expect from what you have learned so far, and also at some of the problems you might encounter on your journey and how you can help yourself to overcome them.

SYNCHRONICITY

Due to the power of attraction in action you may find that you are drawn to and will attract people who have similar beliefs to yourself. You will find that friends and acquaintances to whom you have never spoken about belief systems will start to open up to you, and will be surprised at how many people have the same ideas and ideals as you do. When you start to talk about the work you are doing and the route you are taking, you will find that other people will be encouraged to declare similar views. It will be as though everyone is coming out of the closet!

Another interesting outcome of your newly discovered spiritual awareness will be that strange things will happen – for example, a friend will lend you a book and the next day you will read about it in a magazine and then someone else will suggest you read it. Your guides will be at work here, leading you to helpful information through books, films, magazine articles and people. When two or more people recommend the same book for me to read, or a person for me to meet, I know that this is something I must do. You may also be drawn to have tarot and astrological readings, and will find that here too you will be getting similar messages. These can be helpful in giving you clues about some of the plans that you made for this life, and also for finding out if there is anything that you can do to speed up your healing process.

You will find that you meet the right people at the right time. As an example, a friend of mine is starting a new company; within a week of announcing her plans she had the perfect accountant, lawyer, distribution expert and general manager approach her to help her with her work – all of whom have a similar spiritual awareness to herself. She knows that they have come into her life at just the right time to help her.

DEVELOPING INTUITION

You may find that you have psychic and intuitive gifts that will begin to develop as you become more in tune with the spiritual aspects of life and your own higher self. You could, for example, start to sense energies – become aware of negative and positive energies in buildings and around people; or begin to obtain some knowledge about the future and what is about to happen to yourself or others. You may open up to communication with the spirit world through your meditations, or you might find that you enjoy channelling healing energies directly to people and become a healer.

Developing intuition can lead you to all sorts of interesting pastimes and therapies that you can develop for yourself and to help others. There are many workshops and seminars these days that encourage you to discover and learn more about all these subjects. Reiki is one such subject. It is a great healing practice that you can use for yourself and your family, and is taught worldwide. I suggest you join a local group that practises healing and meditation so that you can develop alongside others. Hearts and Hands has groups around the world; contact this organisation to find out if there is a group in your region, or how to start one of your own if there is not. Contact details can be found at the back of the book.

SOME STUMBLING BLOCKS

As you work with your aspirations you may at times find that there are enormous obstacles on your path. Negative thoughts, feelings and attitudes may come and bite you on your nose as you tread your path! These inner feelings that we despise in ourselves are bound to come up from time to time. Remember that you are not a saint and that there will be times when you may falter. Just dust yourself off; don't take on the guilt but determine to press on.

Here are some of the negative character aspects that can cause you to slip and may create stumbling blocks. The path can certainly get a little slippery at times! To help you if you encounter any of these problems, I have put forward a few suggestions for dealing with them.

Jealousy

This can creep up when you are not looking, and it is uncomfortable both for you and for the person who is the target of your jealousy. I find that I get a feeling rather like a squeezing of my heart centre when someone is jealous of me. It feels restrictive and that's what envy does – it restricts you. The irony of it is that jealousy can come from a source of love. I have known people to get jealous of the time that someone they love spends with another person.

Jealousy often occurs in the many split relationships that exist today – a mother and father separate and the children share the parents' and step-parents' time. It is difficult for a child of any age to accept that their mother or father has a new partner who is taking some of that parent's time. Jealousy that gets out of hand can lead to a lot of emotional pain for all concerned. In some cases it leads to violence.

SUGGESTIONS
The cause of uncontrolled jealousy can be a lack of self-worth or self-esteem, or a dependency on another person for perceived happiness. In the first case, check to see if you value yourself sufficiently and spend some time on healing your self-esteem. If you are jealous of sharing the time of a loved one, then value the time that you do have with them and don't spoil it by pettiness and peevishness, which can drive away the love of the very person you need. If you love them be glad for them that they have found another source of happiness. If you are jealous of someone's success spend some time looking at your own life and seeing how successful *you* are – value your own worth and stop worrying about what other people are doing. You are unique and you offer things to the world that are special too. Value your differences rather than wanting to be the same as someone else.

Apathy

This used to be called sloth in the old days. I wasn't too sure whether to include it but when I looked through my synonym list and saw apathy it rang a bell. We have moved on from the time when work in itself was made a virtue, but there is nothing more soul-destroying – or debilitating even – than being in the state of apathy. 'I don't care' is the creed of someone who is in the state of apathy and it is negative and unhelpful. It can make us lazy and uncaring. As we become lazy and do less, so we lose fulfilment in our life. Our uncaring attitude and lack of interest will upset those around us, irritating them at best and driving them away at worst. No one likes to share time with someone who can't be bothered.

SUGGESTIONS

What can you do when you get caught up in the quagmire of indifference and despondency? Well, apathy shows a distinct lack of interest in life – a sense of boredom. My advice is to find something, no matter what it is, that 'turns you on'; some activity that you have an interest in and can get involved in.

Have a game of golf, go shopping, learn to play a musical instrument, work in the garden, go for a run, go dancing – do whatever you like, but make sure it's something that you participate in. The very act of involvement can stir you out of your negativity. Once you have ignited your passion for one aspect of life you will find that it will spread and your lacklustre feeling will disappear altogether. You could try burning citrus aromatherapy oils in a burner in your home, as this can help lift you up. There are also other alternative therapies, like the Bach Flower Remedies, that can alleviate the dooms and glooms. If your problem persists you may be heading into a full-blown state of depression; if this is the case, I suggest that you look for treatment from a professional.

Materialism

We are living in a material world and it's quite difficult not to get caught up in materialism sometimes. Greed and over-indulgence in acquiring material things is the extreme case of this, making you forego the more subtle pleasures of life for the sake of getting richer or buying more. In general the person who suffers the most is the one who is caught in the trap of consumerism. For them the illusion of happiness is constantly followed by delusion as the realisation hits home that the latest purchase does not in fact bring lasting happiness or contentment. Having possessions in themselves is not wrong, however, and neither is obtaining money, as long as they are not acquired to the detriment of others. I certainly don't think that giving up all your possessions is helpful to anyone in the long run, but I do suggest striking a balance and sharing your good fortune where you can. Unfortunately, there is an imbalance in the world and there is a huge gap between the haves and the have-nots.

SUGGESTIONS

Do you find that you collect possessions? Are you constantly shopping for new clothes? I personally love shopping and I love new clothes like any other woman, but I try to curb any excesses by giving away something whenever I buy a new item. This way someone else other than the shopkeeper and the producer of the goods gets the benefit of my purchasing power. If you tend to hoard money I suggest that you increase your charity donations in proportion to your increasing wealth. Spread your good fortune around.

Worry

Anxiety and worry are normally caused by living in the past or in the future, rather than concentrating on the here and now. Do you spend time worrying about the future, or about mistakes that you perceive you've made in the past? Worry is truly a negative emotion, and it is the greatest time-waster and drainer of energy that I have ever come across. It destroys the moment of now that then becomes the future, so it destroys huge chunks of your life. Disaster may well come upon you one day, but concern yourself with dealing with it then, not now.

SUGGESTIONS

Make sensible provisions to plan for the things that you think you will need in the future if your character and nature demand this, then relax and enjoy your life moment by moment. Whenever you catch yourself worrying, sit down and concentrate on something around you. Focus on something that has no relevance to your problem.

Read a book and immerse yourself in someone else's imagination. Watch television, play a video game, or do whatever else brings you pleasure. When I find myself worrying about a loved one, I send them distance healing (*see pages 81 and 119*). Engaging in such an activity will give you something to do – inactivity is a great breeding ground for pointless anxiety. Practise focusing on the present; cut the cords to the past and surrender the future.

Anger

I had to think twice about whether to add anger to the negative list. You see, I don't always think anger is a negative emotion. I see it as a force from within us that gives us the impetus to push forwards and act. As a force for good, anger:

✧ Enables us to be activists and campaigners who petition and work for the rights of those who have been wronged – to put right the injustices of the world.

✧ Spurs us into action to defend ourselves when we have been unfairly attacked either physically or verbally.

✧ When we are angry at ourselves, it enables us to make changes within and around us for good – to change negative and destructive habits. This type of anger is a spin-off from guilt. It is the emotion that can move us in the direction of reform.

It is when it is directed at another person, community, property or even oneself as aggression that anger can be harmful. Anger is also harmful when it is suppressed for a period of time, for then it boils within us and can harm us emotionally and physically. It can also be caused by irritation with oneself; by one's perceived lack in some way, such as a lack of time, money, achievement or love.

We get angry quite easily these days and I am sure that this is caused by the stresses of life in this century. We are under pressure to achieve more and more in the workplace, to earn more to pay for the goods available to us, and even to put a decent roof over our heads. We are living with a constantly ticking clock, and this creates stress that can lead to anger.

SUGGESTIONS

It is obviously unacceptable to vent your anger at others. Whatever you do try to curb your anger and work on releasing it later. Whenever you feel it coming up count to ten – you just need to get over that first stage when it is out of control. Then, when you have calmed down a little but still feel aggrieved, sit down and work out the real reason for your loss of temper. Check to see if it is yourself that you are really angry with. If you are still simmering either beat a pillow and vent your angst that way, or write down your feelings and then tear up the paper, or even better burn it and let the smoke take away all the emotions as you release them from you for good. I have shared this process with many people and it has great results. If you get angry often take a long look at your lifestyle and check if you are not putting yourself under too much pressure. Ease up a little and find ways to relax.

Keep in mind that it is a long-term investment in time and effort that you are making – very rarely does anyone transform themselves overnight, so be patient with yourself and give yourself credit for any progress you make

REACTIONS FROM FAMILY AND FRIENDS

You will probably find that there will be family members and friends who will be cynical or even want to argue with you about your beliefs. I was quite lucky: although Tony didn't want to join me in meditating and wasn't that sure about healing, he certainly didn't discourage me in any way. However, I have friends who have found that their relationships have changed quite markedly as they have changed their perspective on life – in some cases they have changed irretrievably.

If you have a loving partner you will find that by being tolerant with each other you can continue your loving relationship whatever the differences in your spiritual beliefs. You don't have to practise yoga and meditation to be spiritual and many people follow spiritual tenets and philosophy quietly and unobtrusively by helping others where they can, running businesses with integrity, and carrying on their daily work with care and consideration for others.

There will, however, be some people who will drift away from your orbit and to whom you will find it difficult to relate. Just let it be and accept that there will be new friends coming along with your new interests in life. This can be hard, but we are generally with the people we need for either a learning or a supporting experience – trust that when the need for this has gone a person may walk out of your life.

ROLE MODELS

What can we do to enforce our aspirations? After all, it's all very well to have an ideal in our mind of how we would like to be, but we are living at a rather challenging time when each day brings a new way of knocking us off our perches. I think we can look at people around us for inspiration.

If you can find people who have managed to put these aspirations, these spiritual tenets, into action in their lives, then you have role models that you can use. They have proved that it can be done; that you are not asking the impossible of yourself. You can find role models everywhere – in your family, your workplace or your play world. They can be teachers, theologians, spiritual leaders, artists, politicians, the postman, your husband, your father, your best friend or the cleaning lady at the office. They can show you many of the character traits that you would like to acquire or improve upon, such as patience, strength of character, durability, love, generosity, compassion, integrity, spontaneity, and so on.

This is a time to get out your journal. List all the people you know who have a trait, a way of looking at life, a way of acting out their spiritual credo that impresses you, or who are an inspiration to you in any way.

The next section looks at ways in which you can bring the philosophy that has been described here into your everyday life.

Part II

Bringing Spirituality into Your Daily Life

Being spiritual means being kind and thoughtful to the people you meet every day of your life. It is putting into practice a basic code of love and respect for all life, including yourself. It is about overcoming your fears and negativity and becoming positive about all aspects of your life. It is not about wearing white, taking part in ceremonies or residing in a cave in the Himalayas. You do not need to be a saint to be spiritual.

In this part of the book you can start to see how your new philosophy can come in useful. I will take you through some of the situations you are likely to face in your everyday life and show you how you can use the aspirations, beliefs and powers of our code for living to help you either cope with or overcome your problems. There are no definitive answers, of course, but if you keep in mind the basic principles you will find it easier to make decisions and handle life's challenges.

Life in the twenty-first century is certainly challenging. It is full and pressurised as never before. Job security is a thing of the past in the Western world. Financial institutions are shaky, and can take our pensions and savings down with them if they fail. Fear is rife, whether it be for the future or created by some sudden panic and affecting us today.

With improved communications we are bombarded with facts and visuals of situations around the world and it is easy to become immune to the suffering we see daily. Some of the world's tragedies are caused by natural events, but many are the result of greed, intolerance and the lack of the basic spiritual creed of tolerance and love.

It is a time for change and there is a need to find a different way of living in every sphere of society, from governments to individuals. It is a time to speak up with your choices and your truth. It is a time to activate a spiritual and more caring approach towards people and all other animals, and towards the environment in general. We have seen the devastation of the world by the era of materialism, and it is up to us and our children to change the general attitude of 'not caring' to one of 'caring'. Remembering the way the ripple effect works, we can start by taking our philosophy into our daily lives; eventually we will work on changing the world, but first let's make a start and look at how you treat the person who is closest to you – namely you!

Chapter Seven

LIVING WITH YOURSELF

This chapter is about being spiritual in the way you treat yourself. Being spiritual is a total concept and should reflect on every single aspect of your life. In our enthusiasm to help others and reach out we sometimes forget to look after ourselves. The basis of this is loving and respecting yourself. Before we can effectively help others we need to 'get our own house in order'. There is an old Chinese proverb that goes along these lines:

> If there is peace in the heart there is peace in the home
> If there is peace in the home there is peace in the town
> If there is peace in the town there is peace in the nation
> If there is peace in the nation there is peace in the world

EXPRESSING YOUR FEELINGS

Before you can have a peaceful heart you need to address all your issues and have a thorough understanding of yourself. You also need to be totally honest with yourself about your life. Are you happy with the choices you have made about your partner, home or job? Do you have emotional turbulence from past experiences that you have not dealt with? Do you see yourself with a negative perspective? The first steps of a spiritual journey require you to recognise your strengths and weakness and to work on your inner self, the private and unseen aspect of you, and for this you need total honesty.

We have already seen that lies are weakening and nowhere are they more debilitating than when we are dishonest about our feelings and needs. Do you live a lie? Are you in denial of your feelings or your beliefs? Are you forever saying that things are fine when in fact they are not? Do you know and accept what your emotional needs are and voice them to your family, partner and friends? Or do you say what you think they want to hear? Start to listen to what you are saying and how you respond to those around you. Note when you find yourself saying one thing and feeling another.

Speaking up about your beliefs

It has long been a social custom in the West to avoid the subjects of religion and politics in polite society. In other words, you shouldn't talk about your beliefs in public or even with acquaintances. I have a very rude word to say as a response to this but I'd better not do so here.

In my view it is fine to talk to people about your beliefs. Tony, my husband, once asked me not to talk about my 'spooky' habits when we were at company functions. I complied for a few months but found it hard and would surreptitiously answer questions about my work to the person sitting on the left and right of me at dinners.

Then, one day, during a company function, 12 of us were sitting at a round table. The people sitting around me began to urge me to tell them more and more about energies and how they can be used for healing. In the end everyone apart from my husband and the two people on either side of him were involved in the discussion. He looked up and asked, 'What am I missing out on here?' I just smiled. 'You're not talking spooky talk, are you?' he asked. The other people at the table then shouted him down and told him they were all interested in what I had to say. I therefore 'came out of the closet' and spent the rest of the evening talking to everyone at the table about my beliefs and experiences. Since then Tony has been wonderful and often suggests that people talk to me about the subject.

> **Spiritual principles and beliefs are for daily use, not to be stored away for desperate times and Sundays**

It is very empowering to speak up about your truths – the things you believe in. Obviously, it is not to your advantage to be over-bearing about them and you must let other people express their points of view too, but you have a right to your opinion however alternative and away from the mainstream of public thought it may be. You will be surprised that once you do speak out there will be a lot of people who share your views and have just been shy about declaring them – you will give them courage to also speak up.

What about if you are suppressing your own needs for the sake of loved ones? You don't want to hurt them and want them to be happy, so you keep quiet about your own desires. I used to do this a lot but I eventually found that I couldn't suppress my needs entirely and my resentment would finally come bubbling out, often in the form of anger. One small incident would set me off on an outburst of door-slamming or pot-banging, or would even provoke a verbal onslaught with tears that would stun my husband. He would be utterly amazed at the ferocity of my reaction. What he had received, of course, was a backlash from long-held-back pent-up feelings.

This is definitely not the right way to go. I was lucky because Tony is easy-going, but if you live with someone with a fiery temperament your outburst will just create a similar reaction from your partner. It is far better to explain your feelings and needs as you go along – *gently*, and not with aggression or blame. As soon as you blame someone they immediately feel the need to defend their actions and almost inevitably create an argument.

Once you have explained how you feel you may like to compromise. Here is an example of how this can work. You may feel uncomfortable with your partner's parents. Naturally, your partner gets upset if you criticise them, so you don't like to tell him how you feel. You go along to Sunday lunch at their place every week and feel sick inside and bad the entire time you are there. Tell your partner that you have nothing against their parents but you feel shy with them and would rather not go to visit them every week. Compromise and go sometimes, and allow your partner the freedom of visiting them whenever they wish. The worse thing you can do is to continue with the visits and never show your partner how you feel; the second worse thing is to shout at your partner or criticise their parents or – both!

> Speak out in a kind and considerate manner and explain your feelings; be gentle – this is one of the aspects of love

This was just one example of the tensions that can occur between partners and family members. There are many such instances, and you may find that you get upset quite often. If this is the case look at why you are upset – is there something you need to address within yourself? Here is a quick checklist to help you ascertain if the problem actually lies within you.

✦ Has this situation occurred with other people?

✦ Do you get the feeling that circumstances and people are against you?

✦ Do you feel really bad inside if someone criticises you?

✦ Do you feel that you are always being nagged or criticised?

✦ Do you get feelings of anger for no real reason?

✦ Do you think people are talking about you?

✦ Do you get upset with your partner if they don't include you in everything they do?

If your answer is yes to two or more of these questions, I would say you need to do some work on self-healing. You would seem to have insecurity problems and maybe self-esteem issues that may be the result of some traumatic or painful experiences in your past. These can reflect on your relationships with people and temper the way that you respond to those who are close to you.

WHAT MAKES YOU HAPPY?

Have you ever even considered what makes you truly happy and fulfilled? Spend a few moments listing all the things in your life that give you pleasure, delight or fulfilment. Then list all the things that are wrong in your life. This should not be a list of 'blames on others' but one that relates to the choices you are making that aren't serving you.

By happy I mean having a good, strong feeling inside, and not necessarily fulfilling a desire. For example, you may feel happy on a Saturday night when you've had a few drinks and are sharing fun with friends. You may think that the drink is making you happy – but I wouldn't be surprised if it's the friendship and camaraderie which bring relaxation and laughter that is the true happiness you are feeling.

Once you have made your list, take a look and see how many of the things on the negative side you could change. Now decide what is holding you back from making the changes. Check if it is fear, and see how realistic the fear is before you dismiss a change. Also before making any change, sit with the decision for a couple of weeks, and ask yourself every day if the move is the right one for you. Check if it isn't just that the grass looks greener on the other side, and if the move will truly suit you.

HEALING YOURSELF

Your aspirations include knowing and understanding yourself, and then healing yourself. You need to commit to knowing yourself better and working on the issues that create havoc in your life. The scars of past traumatic experiences are the major causes of disharmony, anguish, depression and disturbed emotions in the present.

It is essential that you spend time getting to know yourself and your problems. Make a note of everything that upsets you and see if there are trends. See if you suffer guilt or resentment, jealousy or fear. Take time to work on these emotions and intend to overcome them. There are many good books and workshops available to assist you in healing your emotions. Find one that suits you and follow the processes that are taught diligently – it's no good saying you want to get better and then not taking the medicine.

I have to warn you that it takes time to heal totally. We are like onions and as we sort out one layer, so the next one comes to the surface. If you have suffered badly in your past it may take a number of months or years before you overcome, or release, all the pent-up emotions of anger, bitterness and fear that are the outcome of the experience. My book, *Heal Yourself*, is a guide to healing and releasing old emotions, and to coping with the resulting anxieties and emotional and mental pain. There are also many other books that show you how you can take your well-being into your own hands (*see page 262*).

Here is another checklist: this will give you some indications of whether you need to work on self-healing.

✧ Do you get jealous of your siblings, children or partner?

✧ Are you frightened of being on your own?

✧ Do you flare up in anger quickly?

✧ Are you nervous of meeting new people?

✧ Do you have any fears or paranoias other than natural fears?

✧ Is your conversation peppered with 'I hate' or 'I can't stand'?

✧ Is there anyone who you still get bad feelings about when you think of them?

If you answer yes to any of the above questions you need to start working on a self-healing programme. These problems will be stopping you from being at peace and need to be addressed before they become severe or affect your health. They will certainly be affecting your harmony, peace and inner happiness, which is your goal.

> The very fact of stepping onto your path and reading this and similar books will have started your healing process

CHOOSING A GOOD PARTNER

Most of us want and need love in our lives to make us feel complete. However, it is essential that you don't jump into the first relationship that comes along and make a commitment to someone who will not allow you to grow your self-esteem. Your self-confidence and self-respect are paramount for your well-being, and under no circumstances do you want to be with someone who threatens them in any way. I know it can be hard when you are on your own. When I was on my own, I can remember many times when I wished that I had someone to share my life with, but it is no good spending your time with someone who brings you down, destroys your peace of mind and threatens your self-reliance and self-love.

I have only one question on this checklist: does the person in your life make you feel good about yourself, and if not, why are you with them?

You may be staying in a relationship with someone who mistreats you or doesn't treat you well for a number of reasons.

✧ They make you feel secure, offering you financial security.

✧ You feel unable to cope without a partner.

✧ They love you.

✧ You are in a habit, a way of life, and accept what comes.

✧ You don't feel you deserve a loving and supportive partner.

✧ You love the person and cannot imagine life without them even though they treat you badly at times.

✧ You have children and they need both parents.

None of these is a truly satisfactory reason to stay with someone if they are abusing you mentally or physically, or if your self-esteem is being driven into the ground by them. Let's take a closer look at each of these points.

Desiring security

What is the point of financial security if you are feeling so bad much of the time? Money does not bring happiness – that's a fact. It may take away a fear, but this is no compensation for a miserable time. Some of the poorest people in the world have found inner happiness and contentment. Ask yourself what is most important to you.

You may actually be lucky enough not to have to make that decision in the long run; you could find financial security through your own endeavours rather than by relying on someone else. I found it quite difficult to give up work and to begin to rely on my husband for financial support, but I have relaxed about this now. If, however, he used this to manipulate me in any way, I would immediately look for a way to be independent again.

Finding it difficult to cope on your own

You may be surprised at how well you can cope if you have to. I have seen people grow immensely because they have been forced to cope with situations that they have been running away from. It is a form of facing your fears, and that always makes you stronger.

It will depend on which culture you come from whether this is a big problem for you. In the West it has become quite normal for a woman or a man to live alone and manage to support themselves. Many women have become better acquainted with technical and home-management issues, and many men have become acquainted with domestic appliances such as cleaning devices and cooking utensils in the home. It is also acceptable for a woman or a man to take part in most social functions and mix in society as a single person. In some cultures, however, a woman is definitely at a disadvantage if she is single. I send love and support to those of you who are in this situation, and say that you may be surprised at where you will find help. Friends and neighbours, brothers and cousins can all help you, and anything has to be better than the unhappiness of a bad relationship.

Needing the love

Maybe you stay with your partner because they say they love you. However, if they don't follow this through with their actions this love is of little value to you.

✧ Do they say they love you yet still treat you badly at times, neglect your needs and trample over your feelings?

✧ Do they repeatedly apologise for their mistreatment of you and vow undying love yet repeat the misuse again and again?

Your partner may well feel great love for you but if they cannot turn this love into continuous and sustained loving action, it is of no use to you. They are most likely suffering themselves and in need of healing. You will have to decide if you want to be the one who tries to heal them, but if they show no dedication to taking their own healing as a serious commitment then I am afraid you will lose the battle. We all have to heal ourselves, and another person can only assist in the process. If your partner shows no sign of seriously working on themselves in order to sort out the problem that causes their erratic and contradictory behaviour, then you are going to continue to have the problems in your life that they create.

Being apathetic

If you know that your relationship isn't good but remain in it nonetheless, you may have become conditioned. Maybe you don't feel you have the energy to change things. Maybe your life has become a habit that you cannot break. Do you sometimes ask yourself 'Is it all worth it?' or 'They're all the same – what's the point of changing?' If the answer is yes, it would seem that you have lost your zeal for life and that the troubles you have encountered have worn you down.

Perhaps you need a new perspective on life – the very fact that you are reading this book shows that you are interested in learning a new way. You will only be able to make the change when you have decided to do so yourself, notwithstanding the pressure and advice given to you, however lovingly, by family, friends or counsellors.

Apathy can be a result of depression or physical illness. Look at yourself closely and check if you are not mentally run down. If you are, try hard to find something to engage your mind. Start a new evening class, buy something new, take up a sport, get a good book to read – anything to break you out of your inertia. Once you have brought some life back into your days you will be in a stronger position to make decisions about your life in total. Once you have raised yourself above your lethargy you may find ways to improve your relationship and breathe fresh life into it. The subject of relationships is discussed further in Chapter 00.

Lacking energy

You may feel apathetic due to low energy. If you are lacking energy because you are physically sick, get yourself checked out by a doctor or alternative therapist who you trust. The wrong food can often cause us to become depleted of energy as food allergies are prevalent these days due to the toxicity of the soil and water supply, and to overuse of chemical pesticides. I get tired and listless if I eat wheat or don't get enough good fresh water. Too much caffeine or alcohol can also be a problem. A naturopath will help you with natural remedies for energy loss and help you with your diet.

MEDITATION TO RELAX

Fear and anxiety can also be debilitating, so look at using meditation to bring you into a calmer state. Here is a short meditation you might like to use when you feel that your anxieties are running away with you.

✧ Find somewhere where you can make yourself comfortable and put on some relaxing music.

✧ Close your eyes.

✧ Focus on your shoulders and upper back. Drop your shoulders.

✧ Breathe in deeply six times – follow your in-breath in through your right nostril and down into your lungs and out through your left nostril.

✧ Breathe in deeply six more times – this time follow your in-breath in through your left nostril and down into your lungs and then out through your right nostril.

✧ Deliberately relax your face and imagine all the lines – especially your frown lines – being eased away by gentle, soothing hands.

✧ Clench and unclench your hands several times.

✧ Clench and unclench your feet several times.

✧ Stretch your spine and imagine light flowing up and down it, loosening the vertebrae and sending light all across your back.

✧ Breathe in deeply six times – follow your in-breath in through your right nostril and down into your lungs and out through your left nostril.

✧ Breathe in deeply six more times – follow your in-breath in through your left nostril and down into your lungs and then out through your right nostril.

✧ Know that you are at peace and surrounded by light – all is well.

Feeling you don't deserve a loving and supportive partner

One of the problems of having low self-esteem is that you may feel you are unworthy of receiving love. You may feel that you deserve a second-rate or dysfunctional relationship that is short of love and tenderness. If this is the case you definitely need to work on your self-acceptance and self-love. Each one of us suffers from this to a certain extent. Lack of self-esteem can manifest itself in many ways, one of them being that it makes you think you are unworthy of consistent love. This will make you accept second best. I don't mean that you deserve a more beautiful, glamorous or handsome partner – I'm talking about having a partner who considers you and your feelings. So how do you improve your self-esteem? This is a big subject in itself and one that I have covered in my book *Heal Yourself*, but here are a few pointers.

> Look for the cause – then
> you can work on the cure

✧ Is the cause the way your mother or father treated you as a child? If it is, it may have been they who had the problem. Maybe they were unable to treat you well because of their own dysfunctions and hurts. Try to forgive them and send them light and love – whether they are living or not their souls can receive healing. This will help you to step into the role of helper rather than feel yourself to be the victim. See Chapter 8 for more on your relationships with your parents.

✧ Do you have low self-esteem because you are a perfectionist and therefore can never live up to your own exacting standards and expectations? Try to be a little more relaxed with yourself. Ask yourself whether you would be so critical if you were your daughter, son or close friend – or whether you would be loving and accepting. See yourself as a dual person – speak to the 'other you', and show love and understanding instead of being critical and dismissive.

✧ Have you had some major setbacks at work? Maybe you have lost a job or been made redundant and feel that you are of no value to society. Unfortunately, this is too common an occurrence these days, but it has nothing to do with the value of a person. You may have lost a job because you were in the wrong role. My first job was a total disaster. I should never have been a secretary – it doesn't suit my temperament or skills at all.

We will be looking at work situations later, so here I'll just say that you need to realise that jobs these days are not for life and that there are actually many other ways of fulfilling your life than working five days a week for another person or organisation. Some of the happiest people I know are those who have accepted redundancy. They have got over the pain and recognised that losing their job was not a sign of inadequacy on their part. They now live much richer and happier lives, pursuing a way of living that they could not have considered if they were still in their old employment.

Whatever the cause of your low self-esteem, don't let it bring you down so low that you don't think you deserve love. *Everyone deserves love.* Remember that we are all created from the same, very loving source. We come from a source of love and that is where we will ultimately return – love should be part of everyone's life, and if your partner cannot give you that love find someone else who can. Definitely do not put up with a relationship that does not give you love because you feel you don't deserve it. You deserve it as much as anyone else. Work on your own outflow of love towards anyone you meet. This practice of giving love will – through the power of attraction – bring love towards you. You can start by treating the cashier at your local supermarket with a smile and a kind word and take it from there.

Loving your partner and being unable to imagine life without them

If you are being mistreated or neglected by someone yet continue to love them, ask yourself if you really do love them, or if you are staying with them for one of the other reasons we have already looked at. Are you in denial about the real reason for staying with them? Are you doing so because you cannot imagine loving someone else? You certainly won't meet another love while you stay with your current partner and continue to be misused.

Having children who need their parents

This is the hardest call of all. You are in a bad relationship and yet you have your duty as a parent to consider. You don't want to harm your children by breaking up their parents. If you have children your measure of how bad your relationship is will be stretched. You will accept more for the sake of the children than you would if you had just your own circumstances to consider. This is inevitable – once we are responsible for children we are vulnerable, and we are not able to follow our whims and fancies; we cannot 'travel light'.

My parents did split up when I was very small as my mother was determined to ensure that I was not brought up with discord and acrimony around me. This worked out well for me, because my mother had a new partner quite soon and I therefore never lacked a father in my life. I wonder how many couples who stay together for the sake of the children really do them a service. I do think that hearing your parents constantly arguing and being torn between them can be very destabilising and harmful. I am sure that having two stable and happy parents, albeit living apart, can be better for children than living with two acrimonious and unhappy ones. Each case is different and each of us must make our own judgement on this. If you are in this situation I suggest you pray and ask for guidance, and hold in your mind the intention of making a decision that is the very best for all concerned.

If you are living with someone who harms you mentally, emotionally or physically, it is essential that you do something to change the situation before you are filled with hatred. Having hatred in your heart is damaging to you on all levels, and most importantly it stunts you spiritually.

Does your relationship serve you?

It is very difficult to keep up your goal of being loving and compassionate if you are living with someone who treats you badly. There is no set yardstick to say what will make a good partner – we all have different needs and our own character will attract different types of people. That is why we should make our own minds up about our choice of life partner. Our friends and family, and even the glossy magazines that offer so much advice in this arena, cannot make the decision for us. I will, however, suggest that you go through the following checklist.

✧ Does your partner's attitude towards you or behaviour towards you frequently cause you emotional pain?

✧ Do they physically harm you?

✧ Do they belittle you frequently in public?

✧ Do they treat you like a possession rather than a sharing partner?

✧ Do they manipulate you so that you fall in with what they want, for example use the children as a tool against you?

✧ Do they dominate you to the extent that you have to follow their wishes?

✧ Are they excessively jealous, to the point of paranoia?

✧ Do they make you feel you are totally inadequate or unlovable?

If the answer is yes to any of these questions I suggest you think long and hard about your relationship – you may have to accept that you have chosen the wrong partner.

If your relationship is just going through a rocky patch, or if you would just like to improve it, you will find some suggestions that might prove helpful in Chapter 10, where we look at relationships and how they function. Do everything you can to improve your situation before you make any big decisions about leaving a relationship – then you will be moving from a position of strength not a place of doubt.

Life is a number of seconds and minutes and each one is precious. Why would you want to take one of those precious minutes and throw it away by allowing yourself to be made unhappy and to be harmed by someone who is not your jailer or owner? Gather your strength and pray for guidance and courage, then make the move that you need to make along your path – allow yourself to walk into a lighter place. Use the powers of manifestation to give you the strength to move to a more loving situation.

What are you looking for in your choice of partner?

Write down a list of attributes or attitudes that you would like in a partner. If you have a partner, make a note of which ones match their characteristics. Here are a few of the typical traits you can list – I leave the more personal ones for you!

✧ Stable and comfortable to be with

✧ Similar interests to mine or at least something in common

✧ Similar ethics and spiritual aspirations to mine

✧ Caring and thoughtful

✧ The same core values as mine

CHOOSING FRIENDS

You are drawn by lust and love to your partners and you inherit your family, whereas you can choose your friends. You should have total control over your choice of friends. If you think that you don't then it would seem that you are in a very controlled environment and need help.

I have always been very lucky in having a number of very close, supportive and loving friends. They are not overbearing and don't try to dominate my life. However, I have known people who have so-called friends who become intrusive with their attention, which can be quite claustrophobic.

As I have already pointed out, you may find that once you are travelling along your spiritual path some of your current friends could feel that a gulf has opened up between you and they may well drop out of your life. As you become more spiritual your energy vibrations change and you start to attract different people. You may also find that some of your friends have very different views and beliefs from yours, and this difference may create a barrier between you. It is quite important that your friends share at least some of your beliefs, otherwise you could find yourself denying your beliefs just for the sake of their friendship. I have friends with whom I share different aspects of my life, but they all have the same core values and credo of life as I do – I truly don't see how we could be friends if they did not.

Don't be afraid to let people go out of your life. People come and go in this day and age, and friends are not committed to each other for life – they may be around to see you through a particular time or to share some important experiences with you. After a time they may need to move on and leave your immediate circle. Just let them go if they wish to leave. There will be new friends waiting to join you and share the next stage of your life. Of course, loyalty is important and you can always keep the door open for an old friend in need. One of life's great pleasures is helping someone you love.

Keep a rein on your expectations from friends and don't demand too much of them. If you do expect too much from someone there is a chance that they will not be able to live up to your expectations, and you will feel let down and they will feel guilty. Guilt is not a good bedfellow with friendship – although I know several people who like to make their friends feel guilty and in their debt. Low expectations and lots of love are a better combination as the basis of a good friendship.

CHOOSING YOUR WORK

Another aspect of loving and respecting yourself is making sure you are doing work that makes you feel good. I know that we don't all have a vocation and sometimes we can seem to drift into jobs, but it is important that we don't get stuck in a rut for too long doing something that upsets us at a deep level – that is out of kilter with our soul and its needs. I think most people have a dream somewhere in their psyche, and you need to identify your job role as soon as possible to be truly happy.

THE WORST SCENARIO

✧ Your job doesn't really suit you.

✧ You feel depressed every morning.

✦ You are committed to a lifestyle that demands you stay with your current job.

✦ Your job is too difficult for you.

✦ Your job makes you feel inadequate.

✦ The nature of your work disturbs you.

✦ Your job requires you to lie and be deceitful.

✦ You dislike many of your work colleagues.

✦ You are underpaid and overworked.

✦ Your job completely stresses you out and exhausts you.

Do any of the above statements apply to you?

THE BEST SITUATION

✦ Your job fulfils you.

✦ You are happy to go to work most days.

✦ You feel needed and of value at work.

✦ You enjoy the companionship of your colleagues.

✦ You feel you are benefiting humanity or the world in some way, no matter how small.

✦ Your job pays you enough for you to meet your needs.

✦ Your job uses your skills and suits your temperament.

Remember your goal – inner peace and contentment. It would be impossible to gain this objective if you were totally miserable in your work. As with a partner, there is no such thing as a perfect job, but if the negative aspects outweigh the positive ones, think about having a change. Maybe you can alter your role within your current workplace to something that suits your skills and temperament. There is nothing worse than being a square peg in a round hole. It will make you feel continually inadequate and frustrated. Your employers should pick this up, but for a number of reasons they may not do so – it will be up to you to speak up and see what you can do to find a suitable role. I have done jobs in my past that weren't suitable for me and they made me thoroughly miserable.

If you are good with people find a job that allows you to meet them and develop your communication skills. If you love children find a job working with them. I have a friend who is great with children of all ages and she comes alive when she is with them or even talks about them, yet she has spent the last few years of her life working in a bank. It is no wonder that she feels incomplete and frustrated with her life. She will never be truly happy until she follows her dream and steps onto the right path. It will take courage, as her job pays quite well and she, like most of us, has financial commitments. However, I truly believe that if you are doing the job that you planned to do before you came to Earth this time, there will be enough money and you will manage. The universe has a habit of looking after us when we are doing the work we should be doing.

Also be prepared to change from time to time – this will keep you fresh and also make your life more interesting and challenging. Most of us grow with challenges and new environments and by changing your job role, even if not necessarily your company, from time to time, you will have a more stimulating life.

Coping with stress

Some jobs are extremely stressful; in fact, these days of strong competition and difficult economies put employers and employees under more and more pressure to succeed. There is an increasing incidence of burn-out among people in our businesses and schools. It is therefore important to recognise the stress that comes with your job – you need to identify the stress that you cause yourself, and the stress that is inherent to the position you hold. For example, if you are a competitive person and enjoy the hunt of the chase that comes with sales, you may well find that the stress of a highly pressurised sales position raises your adrenalin levels and gives you a buzz that you enjoy. On the other hand, if you prefer to work with your brain and find competition upsetting, enjoy the complexities of accounting or unravelling computer technology and keep away from a sales position with demanding targets.

Sometimes we are catapulted away from a stressful job. Someone I know worked for years for the same company. He was very successful, and achieved all his targets. He was fine until he was promoted to manager. In that position he was faced with the stresses of getting other people to achieve targets and goals and he realised that this was another ball game. He became increasingly stressed and unhappy but couldn't find the courage to walk away from a 'safe' job. Fortunately for him, the company was taken over and in the ensuing reorganisation he was made redundant. This was a great gift for him because he then started to work for himself doing all the jobs that he enjoyed. He earned enough to get by and increased his quality of life immediately.

The wrong job can in itself cause you stress. As was the case with my friend described above, being in a job for which you have had inadequate training can be a cause of stress. Your life will be nothing but a struggle if you are learning the job as well as trying to cope with deadlines and pressures. If you don't feel you have been properly trained or think that you need further qualifications to accomplish the role successfully, be honest and ask for training from your employer. If you feel that your educational qualifications are not good enough to get you a job that will fulfil you, consider a mature graduate position at university or evening classes.

I have a friend who completely changed direction when he was around 40 years of age. He had been a medical illustrator and decided to move into graphic design because he felt this would give him greater scope to fulfil his creative needs. He went back to university to take a degree in graphic design, and after a short time of rehabilitation found himself thoroughly enjoying the study and fulfilled by the nature of the work. It's never too late to learn new skills – at the grand age of 82, my mother is taking computer classes and is now a whiz on the Internet!

Apart from finding a good partner to share your life I think that doing the work that suits you best is the most important aspect of loving and caring for yourself. It is walking your talk to acknowledge what you need to be doing to make you feel happy. If you deny yourself this you are being dishonest, unloving and disrespectful to yourself. The wrong job can be a great stumbling block on your spiritual path.

> Stress expresses itself with hurtful
> words and impatient attitudes

GIVING YOURSELF TIME

Trying to beat the clock is one of the causes of stress and its attendant emotions of frustration, anger and tetchiness. It's very difficult to keep calm and relaxed, to smile and be pleasant to everyone around you, when you are desperately trying to get a job finished before time runs out, or chasing an appointment with the traffic conspiring against you. You want to keep a friendly demeanour and keep yourself cool? Then don't over-crowd your diary and allow plenty of time for travelling to your next meeting.

This applies equally to you whether you are a mother with

children at school or a business executive. It means that from time to time you will have to say no. You have to learn to turn down invitations, withstand pressure from colleagues to take on extra projects, and be honest with your boss about the realities of timescales and your ability to meet them. It's difficult in a work environment, as we want to give a good impression by saying that we can always do something. However, the cost is often high and it really doesn't create the best impression to be late, miss deadlines or become antisocial because you cannot meet the commitments you have taken on.

While writing this book I have had to be disciplined about the number of people I see, and it is difficult. I don't like turning people down, especially those I know well, but if I don't keep to my line I shall miss the window of time that I have allocated and then the pressure will really be on. I personally don't work so well when I feel sick inside from worry about whether I will finish my work on time.

Managing unreliability

Some people are too laid-back and arrive late for everything. This is not a great way to be and it shows a lack of consideration for other people. You are effectively saying that your time is more precious than theirs – or that you think so little of the other person that you don't care if they have to sit around waiting for you.

Unreliable people are extremely irritating and can create disharmony wherever they function. If you have a colleague or friend who is unreliable in respect of their timekeeping or their promises how do you react to them? Don't they make you irritable and eventually angry? Once we start to raise negative emotions around us we will be affected by these bad vibrations; we will be surrounded by bad atmosphere and lose people's trust. Whether this occurs in the workplace or in a family context, it makes life extremely difficult for everyone.

Check your motives when you volunteer or accept responsibility for something. It is wonderful to offer to do things for people, but only do so if you can manage them. Sometimes we offer to do things for others because we either want to be liked or want the status that being the organiser brings. Say yes only if you want to help and have the time to do so, because if you fail to keep your promise you will hurt yourself as well as others. This applies to taking on a job, offering to do voluntary work, taking other people's children to school, giving people a lift to work or accepting business contracts.

Managing your time

In business circles a few years ago it was very popular to have a personal organiser, and time management was a much-used catchphrase. Very often we can do more and achieve more if we are more effective with the time we have available. I have a policy that works well for me. I allocate slices of time for the various aspects of my life.

I reserve weekends for family, allocate weeks at a time to write, put aside whole days for healing and allow time for holidays. I allow a short time at the beginning of each of my working days for answering emails, and reserve lunchtimes for meeting friends. I am quite strict about keeping to the time spaces I allocate for each event, as experience has taught me that this is necessary. In the past I rushed about and my days were totally chaotic, with a mixture of answering mail, taking phone calls, trying to help people with healing sessions in between, and upsetting my family by working into the night.

Find the way that suits you but consider time allocation. It will also help you to relax more if you know that every job has a time slot and that they will all be done in turn. It can also be a good habit to work out your priorities, decide which is the most important task and then just concentrate on this until it is finished. One of my worst habits is that I jump about from job to job and I have found that it really helps me to have a priority list.

Here are a few suggestions that may help you to manage your time effectively.

✧ Give yourself time when taking a journey – add 50 per cent extra time to allow for bad traffic and unreliable transport.

✧ Learn to say, 'No, sorry.' Don't make promises to do something when you already have a full agenda.

✧ Avoid taking on projects with deadlines that you are not completely confident you can meet.

✧ Prioritise your time.

✧ Be realistic – don't wish yourself into a situation. Be honest with yourself and others about your ability to meet your commitments.

✧ If you are late or have let someone down take responsibility – don't blame others. Your honesty and apologies at this point can mitigate the situation, but if you continue to make excuses you compound the negative vibes.

✧ Release your ego.

THE QUESTION OF PROSPERITY

In this chapter I am discussing ways in which you can be spiritual in your daily life and treat yourself well. I therefore need to address the question of wealth and income. I meet a lot of people who struggle to follow a spiritual path and also create an income for either themselves alone or for their families. One of the reasons why they struggle is that they have often given up their main career and moved towards what would seem to be a more 'spiritual' occupation.

I recently met a banker who gave up the corporate life to become a yoga teacher. The difference in her income is immense, and although she felt good about her teaching she also felt the lack of income. She also didn't find teaching yoga full-time as fulfilling as she had first thought it would be. She has now come to a compromise and returned to banking, but has taken a less stressful position and continues to give her yoga classes in the evenings and at weekends. By doing this, she has solved her income problem and I am sure that once she has adjusted to being back in the corporate world she will have a more balanced life.

We do not need to forsake all to become spiritual

There is nothing 'unspiritual' about being a banker or a shop assistant or a commodities dealer – it is how you are in yourself and the way you interact with those around you that makes you spiritual. It is important that you enjoy your work and that it makes you happy, but there is no need to give up a job just because you are 'on your path'. The challenge for us at this time is to be spiritual in the real world, not to run off to the mountains and find the nearest cave. We may do this for a while to give us an opportunity to evaluate ourselves and our lives, but I don't recommend it as a life purpose. So, on this basis you can still keep an income and prosper.

If you have decided that being a carer, volunteer or therapist is the way you need to go, then you will have to face the consequences of earning a low income. One point that I would make is that there seems to be a stigma placed upon earning an income from healthcare or alternative therapies such as energy healing. I have had my own problems with taking payment for healing, but

I would say that everyone deserves to be recompensed for their time, experience and expenses.

It takes a long time for a healer or therapist to become quali-fied and experienced enough to put themselves forward to work with the public – it is similar to the way a doctor spends years at university studying before they can practise. There is no reason, therefore, why a healing therapist should not be rewarded for their time and work. You should be able to prosper without guilt and still be spiritual.

CONSIDERING YOUR LIFESTYLE

One of the early realisations that comes to us when we start along our path is that we cherish life; we therefore begin to look after ourselves a little better than before. Once you see the true value of your life on Earth and why you are here, it makes sense to keep your body in better shape and therefore able to cope with all the challenges that you are likely to face on your journey. You also want to achieve your goals and missions and this is easier to manage with good health. You may therefore like to consider your lifestyle and see if there are any areas where you could improve your health and well-being by dropping a few habits that challenge your health, such as smoking, excessive drinking, late nights and drugs.

I personally think that if you can manage your excesses and ensure that you treat yourself well and with care, then there is no need to change your lifestyle dramatically. It is your personal choice, however, and you must do what feels right for you. Let's just look at some aspects of how we treat our bodies and see if you can bring in some moderation and improve your well-being by a few changes of attitude and approach.

Meditation

I have already mentioned meditation in this book. It is a very useful tool and can help in many aspects of your life. You can use it to know yourself better, or to connect to God, the angels and your spirit guides; it can also be good for your health as it helps you to relax both physically and mentally. Make it one of your regular life routines. You can do it in bed when you wake up in the morning, or in the middle of the night, or just for a few minutes sitting in your favourite chair – you just need quiet surroundings and the intention to stop for the benefit of your spiritual development and physical well-being. It is also the state you need to enter to send distance healing. You can therefore focus on all these aspects while you are meditating:

✦ Relaxing your physical and mental bodies

✦ Connecting to your higher self

✦ Connecting to God and the divine

✦ Sending light and love to humanity and the world

There are many different styles and types of meditation, but they all help your health and well-being. I practise a style called guided visualisation, through which we follow simple steps read by someone. To assist your meditation and enable you to send distance healing, I have written a booklet and recorded CDs which you can purchase from my organisation, Hearts and Hands. We have an established network of meditation and distance-healing groups, and if you are interested in forming a group or joining an existing one please get in touch with us. Contact details can be found at the back of the book.

MEDITATION FOR CREATING A SPIRITUAL CONNECTION

Here is a meditation that you can use to make a spiritual connection. Remember to ground yourself first (*see page 24*).

✧ Close your eyes and breathe in deeply four times.

✧ Drop your shoulders and relax your arms, legs and entire body.

✧ Say: 'I call in the angels to surround me, protecting me with their love.'

✧ Say: 'I call in the archangels above and below me, with their great wings outstretched creating a canopy of love and protection.'

✧ Say: 'I call in God's divine love and see it stream through as light pouring down and filling me with the love and compassion of my divine creator.'

✧ See and sense a great light filling you and spilling over and around you. Feel the great love of God filling every cell of your body. Feel your heart centre fill to overflowing with love.

✧ Send this love outwards in great beams of light to every place and every single person on Earth who needs love.

✧ See roots from your feet stretching down into the earth and feel your connection with Mother Earth. Through your spirit and soul feel the oneness of all souls, all creation and God. Through your body feel the oneness with Mother Earth and all of nature.

✧ Say your own personal prayer of thanksgiving.

Meditation and prayer are personal matters and can be done in any manner that suits you. They are a very important part of a spiritual process as they offer you the facility to step out of the reality of your physical body and the everyday world in which we live. They give you time to focus on the higher presence of your creator and your own spiritual aspect. Try to find some time every day – even if it is just a few minutes – to make this connection. You will find that it is the quickest and most effective way to bring peace to your innermost being.

A SIMPLE MEDITATION

Here is a quick and simple meditation that will allow you to start the day with a spiritual connection and to send healing to all.

✧ Stand with your arms outstretched above your head, opened wide.

✧ Embrace the light of the sun, the moon and the universe.

✧ Call in the love and light of God.

✧ Bring this loving energy into your heart: bring your hands to your heart centre (in the centre of your chest) and hold them there for a minute as you capture the love of the universe in your heart.

✧ Now open your arms and with your palms facing inwards imagine you hold the Earth; let the love flow into every living thing on Earth. You are healing the planet, humanity and every animal, bird and plant – everything that lives.

✧ If you know anyone who is in need of help, visualise them between your hands.

Do I need to be a vegetarian?

People have often asked me whether they need to change their lifestyle, become vegetarians, give up alcohol and so on, if they want to be spiritual. I feel that any changes in your lifestyle will come as your choice following your determination and intention to follow the credo and beliefs of a spiritual person. This will follow whatever spiritual path you take – whether it be the Christian faith, Buddhism or some other form of belief.

Once you start to see the connection between humanity and animals and open yourself to a deeper respect and love for them, there is a very high possibility that you will no longer wish to eat meat. This doesn't mean you *have* to become a vegetarian. Personally, I couldn't bear eating an animal and the thought of putting flesh into my mouth has become abhorrent to me. This was my choice, and it is more to do with my feelings than with my beliefs.

Once you start to think about animals and how they are treated it is quite natural to become more choosy about eating them and to move towards eating organic meat and other produce. If you do decide to become a vegetarian, keep a check on how you feel and how it works for you. There are people who seem to need some form of animal protein and you may be one of these – if you find that you just don't feel good on a full vegetarian diet (that is, a diet with no meat, fish or fowl), consider reintroducing fish. Several of my friends feel this is a good compromise. You might find it helpful to read the book *Eat Right for Your Type* by Dr Peter D'Adamo, which argues convincingly that different blood types need different foods. This principle holds true for all the people I know who have checked their food preferences and allergies against their blood type.

Can you drink alcohol?

You will find that as you meditate and spend more time accessing the light energies of the universe you will be unable to drink very much alcohol. I have certainly found this to be the case. I lost my tolerance for alcohol and now can only take one or two drinks before I start to feel light-headed and often quite uncomfortable. I still enjoy a drink, however, and it helps me to relax in a social environment.

I will always let my own body and its messages be my guide to whether I should stop drinking alcohol completely or not. I have been through times of abstinence and these have been at the suggestion of my spirit guides and had more to do with detoxification. I am not too keen on the idea of dos and don'ts as I believe that we are on a personal path – that it is up to each one of us to decide how many, if any, alcoholic drinks we can take, and whether they serve us or not. Interestingly, my guides once showed me pictures of my aura: one showed what my aura looked like when I had eaten sugar, the other when I had taken a drink. My aura was disturbed and affected the most by sugar, which is sad for someone with a sweet tooth – a chocoholic like me!

Having enough sleep

Getting an adequate amount of sleep is just good common sense. I feel just as groggy from sleep deprivation as I do if I have too many drinks. My body simply doesn't like too many late nights. If you can get a few early nights your body will certainly appreciate it.

Night-time is when we engage in astral travel and do all sorts of good deeds in the spirit world. You may sometimes wake up after seven hours of sleep and yet feel very tired and reluctant to open your eyes. This can be because you have some unfinished business to complete in the astral planes. When this happens to me I just take the first opportunity to close my eyes and have a nap – after just a few minutes the tiredness leaves me and I am then fine to get on with the day.

Dealing with insomnia

You may be one of the unfortunates who suffer from insomnia. If you have difficulty getting to sleep, check that you are not eating or drinking something that is preventing you from sleeping, such as alcohol, caffeine in tea or coffee, chocolate, cheese, and so on. If your head is spinning with all your anxieties and troubles, try drinking a cup of chamomile tea before bedtime; while you are in bed close your eyes with the intention of meditating.

Start to send healing to those on your healing list – this sometimes works like counting sheep; it takes your mind away from your own woes, and while doing good for those receiving the energies may also lull you to sleep. If you wake in the night you could try the same thing. When you meditate in the middle of the night you may get messages from your spirit guides – they can often come through to you at night-time, when you are faced with few distractions.

At one period in my life I was being woken regularly at 2 p.m. with messages, and I soon learned to keep a pad and pen at the side of my bed.

DREAMS AND ASPIRATIONS

We all have some dreams and aspirations, and I have covered spiritual aspirations quite extensively in this book. Dreams go side by side with hope, which is the fuel of life. You will find that as you start your journey your dreams may come into strong focus.

Your personal hopes and dreams for your future are very likely connected to your life's purpose. If, therefore, you have a great urge to travel, take up a new interest, start a new career, meet a certain person, or visit a specific country, city or sacred site then follow your dream.

I have noticed that many would-be healers (of any kind) are very nervous of stepping forwards and getting training, or once trained are reluctant to put their skills into practice. They say they have some unknown fear that seems to stop them. Very often this is because they have been healers in the past and have suffered terribly because of their work. Many cultures have a history of torturing and persecuting healers and spiritual teachers. In fact, at one time if you were to be a spiritual teacher bringing in a new message to humanity you were doomed to martyrdom. I am so pleased that this is no longer the case in

Western society! If you have unknown fears about starting new ventures, professions or skills, meditate on them and consciously release all ties to the past and all fears associated with past experiences.

> Fear is the stumbling block
> on the path to our dreams

MEDITATION TO LET GO OF LINKS TO PAST PAINFUL EXPERIENCES

In this meditation you can look at your fears, and then visualise yourself overcoming them by seeing yourself actually doing the thing that you fear. If a fear is the result of abuse or physical attack from the past, you can use your imagination to give yourself the strength to overcome your attacker or tormentor. If you are prone to panic attacks check that you can cope with this process. If not then look for professional guidance and consider regression and hypnosis as treatments. Also pray for help to overcome your problem and put out a strong intention to be the master rather than the victim of the past.

✧ Prepare yourself for meditation: relax, ground yourself (*see page 24*) and call in your angels.

✧ Visualise yourself at the base of a mountain. You see a trail clearly marked out on its side with stakes set into the rock. You can see beautiful beings waiting at the side of the path – these are the helpers who will assist you. One steps forwards and introduces herself as your guide.

✧ She strides along in front of you – showing you the way. She is confident and obviously knows her way well and you follow in her footsteps.

❖ You feel strong and confident and you start to climb – it's easy at first and you make good progress. You are filled with enthusiasm for this new challenge.

❖ Gradually the climb becomes harder and the path is steeper, but your guide steps forwards and takes your arm and helps you along.

❖ Suddenly you are faced with a major blockage on the path. Your guide stops and tells you that you alone can clear the obstacle. It will move if you have the courage and the determination to face it – it represents one of your greatest fears. Only you know what that fear is and only you can clear it.

❖ Decide what you are going to do to overcome the obstacle. Visualise yourself doing whatever it is you fear to do. See your-self as a great success. See yourself as strong and fearless. Once you have decided on your plan you find you have the strength to step forwards. As you do so you see the obstacle fade; you stride confidently into it and it disappears.

❖ You feel stronger now; overcoming your fear has made you more powerful.

❖ You continue up the mountain, and from time to time your path is blocked by another of your fears.

❖ Take your time and make your plans – be strong with your inten-tion to let go of fear and step forwards.

❖ Eventually you will reach the top of the mountain, but go as far as feels right for you on this occasion – you can come back any time and continue.

❖ Your guide will take you off the mountain and back into your room when you are ready.

Once you have cleared away your fears you can use the powers of manifestation and creation that I have already introduced you to (*see Chapter 5*). Start now by writing down all those dreams and ideas that you have never had the courage to follow; make your intentions clear by starting a plan of how you are going to fulfil them in your journal.

ACHIEVING BALANCE

Many of the problems we face in life stem from being out of balance. Whenever we are faced with extremes our lives get out of kilter. When this happens we have difficulty in coping and our emotions are likely to flow out of control. At this point we start to affect those around us and to challenge their balance too.

Imagine that you are a member of a great acrobatic act. For each person to be safe, for the entire group to be in harmony, every member has to work on their own stability, and this will affect the stability of the group. The group can be your family or your work team. If one member spirals out of control everyone is affected. The individual who adopts negative behaviour patterns will create difficult atmospheres and hurt those around them. We have all experienced the outpourings of someone who is suffering pain, and we have felt their anger. Whether the group in which we operate becomes destabilised will depend on how we react to this anger. If we react with anger ourselves, everyone will be affected due to the ripple effect.

The most effective way of changing the equilibrium of the group is by working on your own balance. By taking a positive attitude and looking at yourself in a clear and dispassionate way, you will see where you are out of balance. What can throw you off balance? Here are examples of some of the challenges to your balance you may face and tips for dealing with them.

Fears, anxieties and paranoia

These will eventually cause physical problems, such as headaches and worse. They will prevent you from reaching your goals, making the most of your life and finding peace. Fear is your greatest challenge.

TIPS:

✧ Gather your courage, and pray for help to face your fears.

✧ Meditate, look for the root cause and practise facing your fears in your meditations before you face them physically. Use the meditation on page 173 to help you overcome your fears in your mind. Use this as preparation work for the real thing.

✧ Once you have overcome your fears in your meditation – in your imagination – do the things in real life that you fear the most.

✧ Get help from counsellors or therapists – maybe your fears are based in past-life experiences, in which case a visit to a past-life therapist could be helpful.

✧ Most of our anxieties come from worrying about what is going to happen. Deliberately stop from time to time in your day and think about what is happening to you at the present moment. Enjoy the moment and think about now, not the past or the future. Make it a habit to stop and be present. Meditation will help you with this. Reading, or fully participating in a sport or in anything that makes you focus on the present, will also encourage you to engage with the present.

Lack of love or acceptance of yourself

This will lead to low self-esteem and will prevent you from reaching your full potential. It will inhibit you in both your personal and your work relationships.

TIPS:

✧ Make a promise to yourself that you will start working on a positive perspective of yourself.

✧ Join a group of like-minded people and gain their support.

✧ Forgive anyone who may have caused your low self-regard.

✧ If your lack of self-love is caused by guilt, forgive yourself, take note of the lesson learned and then move on with your life.

✧ Get a new look – a new hairstyle, some new clothes – and make a fresh start with this new persona. See yourself as someone who deserves love and care – start by loving and caring for yourself.

✧ Get to the gym and get your body into shape – this will also help with your self-esteem and the exercise will raise your energy levels.

✧ In your prayers and meditation speak to God. He will always love you without any conditions, without caring what you have done and what you feel about yourself. He sees you only through the eyes of love.

Lack of tolerance and compassion for others

If you show these feelings you will become alienated from others and particularly those who are close to you. Your antagonism will create waves around you that will have an effect on you too. If you have to work with someone who is completely negative and insufferable, keep away from them as much as you can.

TIPS:

✧ Try to see the good points in everyone. Accept that they cannot be perfect. Concentrate on the good and try to ignore the bad.

✧ Try to understand why others are the way they are – what experiences have they gone through to make them as they are.

✧ Allow for the differences – each race, culture and even family has different ways of doing things. Allow for these differences and accept rather than condemn them.

✧ Consider the fact that every one of us will see things in different ways – who is to judge what is right and what is wrong? Even with clothes we all have our own preferences – this applies to everything in life.

✧ Open yourself to compassion by helping those who are in difficult situations – for instance, do hospice work, or help children in need. This will open your eyes and heart to the suffering of others.

✧ Step into the shoes of the other person. By feeling the fears of others and empathising with them you can open your heart and compassion will move in.

Holding grudges, bitterness and lack of forgiveness

Physically, this will often manifest as problems with your gall bladder as the bitterness gathers and your digestive system becomes over-acidic. Spiritually, there is no doubt that it holds you back.

TIPS:

✧ Give yourself time to grieve and heal after any major injustice or harm has been done to you or your loved ones. The time you take to heal will vary depending on the level of harm that has been done, but don't let years pass before you start to work on your full healing.

✧ Full healing will only take place for you when you have forgiven the person or persons responsible for your pain.

✧ Revenge is not sweet – justice can salve the wounds but it will not totally heal you.

✧ If necessary, use your hurt and turn it into action – for instance, if it is appropriate, you can campaign to stop the same problem occurring for others.

❖ Remember the person who is most harmed by lack of forgiveness is you. Let go of the past as an act of caring for yourself.

Too much work and not enough relaxation

This is a very common cause of imbalance in our lives. I gather that we work the longest hours in the world in the United States and Britain. Hard work is admirable, and dedication to your work, cause or family is wonderful, but not when it starts to harm your health or well-being. Too many hours spent in the workplace can cause harm not only to your health but also to the stability of your personal relationships.

TIPS:

❖ Ask yourself why you are working such long hours. Is it the policy of your company? If this is the case, weigh up the cost to you in health and social terms. Is it because you are struggling with a workload? Are you fully trained for the work you do? Are you too proud to ask for help? Could you manage your time better?

❖ Consider your free time and rest as your right. You need to take time for fun to bring on the laughter that will help you to unwind on all levels.

❖ See yourself as battery driven. Your time away from work is your time to recharge the battery – if you don't recharge you will stop completely and then no work will get done.

❖ Deliberately create interests that will draw you towards them. Take up a pursuit or sport that makes you excited and keen to participate.

❖ Realise that your body needs exercise and fresh air to operate well. Make sure there is enough of both available to keep you going.

❖ Take time for your spiritual aspect, otherwise it will be drowned out by your working persona and you will find that your inner contentment will continue to be elusive.

Giving too much

This is a common problem particularly for mothers of small children or family carers, who can find their entire days taken over by the demands of their children or a sick relative, leaving no time for care and attention to themselves. Eventually, tiredness and low self-esteem can take over and cause illness and resentment. It is wonderful to help others, but you must also take time for yourself.

TIPS:

✧ If you are a carer find a local association that provides care for the carers.

✧ Take time out each week for your own pursuits or for pampering yourself. Get an aromatherapy massage, take a trip to the cinema or engage in a sport activity – do whatever gives you the most satisfaction and happiness. You will be far more capable – physically, mentally and emotionally – of helping others if you have taken some time for yourself.

✧ Make sure you protect yourself energetically when you are with people or children who are needy, since they will take your energy from you. See yourself surrounded by a huge bubble of white light and know that only love can move through this bubble. This will ensure that your personal energy will not be drained by their needs. Give of your love and attention, but not of your personal life stream.

Too much time spent indoors

This will cause toxicity in your system, particularly if you work close to computers and in a large office. You will become fuggy-headed and start to lose energy.

TIPS:

◇ We all need fresh air and if you cannot get this at your workplace you need to find time to walk outside. Maybe you can go for walks at lunchtime or after work.

◇ The best antidote is a walk in woods or by the sea, as the energies are much stronger and more beneficial there than in city streets. However, any fresh air is better than nothing – even the air in the streets of Hong Kong, New York or London!

◇ We all need exercise to keep our bodies working well so any sporting pastime that you can take up outdoors will help.

◇ Sunlight has been much maligned over the last few years due to global warming and ozone layer problems. However, we do need sunshine and there are many people who actually get sick if they don't get enough of it. As long as you don't over-expose yourself, short periods in the sun are extremely good for you on all levels.

◇ I find a walk in the country an exceptionally spiritual experience. As I become closer to nature so I draw nearer to God. You can enjoy a walking meditation where you just align your mind to the beauty around you and let yourself become assimilated with your surroundings.

Too much attention to your body and image

We are more than just our physical body and if we spend too much of our time and energy focusing on our image and our body's appearance we become spiritually out of balance. I don't mean that you should not take care of your appearance – just that a preoccupation with your image is not healthy. Do you look in the mirror every time you pass one? Are you preoccupied with your body? Have you ever been called a hypochondriac? Do you spend an inordinate amount of time reading fashion magazines? Do you become depressed if you put on a couple of pounds? If you answer yes to a couple of these questions, read on. Sure, it's good to be aware of your image and to look after your body, but you have probably gone too far and may be out of balance in this respect. When this aspect of your life gets too far out of hand you could be heading towards eating disorders.

TIPS:

✧ Understand that your body is the vehicle that carries your spiritual being. It is not alone and is only part of the entire being that is you.

✧ Through meditation you can connect with the higher self and see your physical body in perspective.

✧ Make it your intention that your spirit and mind will be as important to your being as your body and its needs. This way of thinking can also help you to overcome addictions and bad eating habits.

✧ Spend more time thinking of others, particularly those who are worse off than you are and in need of help. Where possible physically help them – this will help balance a self-preoccupation.

Remember that your goal is inner happiness and peace

Here is a checklist to remind you of the things that will help you to achieve inner happiness and peace.

✧ Understand yourself and others.

✧ Express and release your feelings and emotions without harming others.

✧ Handle stress and anxiety.

✧ Make your choices honestly and truthfully.

✧ Develop an inner knowledge of your needs.

✧ Feel the connectedness of all living beings.

✧ Communicate to your God-sense/your divine self, and draw love from this connection.

✧ Heal the past with forgiveness.

✧ Live in the present and enjoy it.

✧ Develop a positive attitude to life and yourself.

✧ Take responsibility for yourself and all that happens for you and to you.

✧ Love yourself and others unconditionally, without judgement.

If this list is too long for you, just concentrate on the last point!

In the following chapters I will give you further examples of how you can bring your spiritual beliefs into everyday situations. Being a role model is infectious, and the love you give yourself and others will spread like ripples until the entire world is affected.

> Spiritual guidance helps us work through
> the challenges, great and small, that we are
> faced with every day of our lives

Chapter Eight

YOU AND YOUR PARENTS

It is through our experiences and challenges in life that we get opportunities to grow spiritually. Family situations can provide us with testing times with our aspirations. We will start here by looking at how we can bring our new values into solving and overcoming some of the problems we may have with our parents.

> Our family members provide us with challenges we cannot avoid

I can hear some of you groaning as we begin to look at family relationships. These can be the hardest things that you have to cope with in your life, and very often they are the things that leave the most lasting impressions on you and cause you the most harm. However, looked at from a positive perspective they offer you the greatest opportunities to learn and grow spiritually.

They teach you how to forgive, be tolerant, share and be strong enough to stand up for yourself.

The way we are treated in our early years will dominate the attitudes that we will take out into the world. If we have been loved and treated well we will start life with a stronger base than if we have not. If every woman loved her child and showed it her love there would be little need for therapists and healers – that is how important the mother/child relationship is. So let's look at the different relationships that our families offer and some of the scenarios that you may have had to handle, and see how your spiritual beliefs and teachings can help you with the sometimes daunting challenges. We start with your parents – your attitudes towards them and their treatment of you.

DO YOU THINK YOUR PARENTS LOVED YOU?

Whether your parents are alive or dead you will still be affected by the question of whether you think they love you. You notice that I say 'think' they love you as it is of course your perception of this that counts for you. They may have loved you very much indeed but if you feel they didn't we need to start from that point. There are therefore two scenarios here. In the first one, your parents may have loved you but were unable to show it – or show it to your satisfaction. In the second one, they did not love you at all.

Look at your own situation – which of these scenarios applies to you? Look back long and hard into the past. Be sure of your answer: I know several families where the children are loved, and tenderness and care have always been shown to them, yet they still think they were or are not loved. Their perspective is skewed because they are looking to pass on blame for their own dysfunctions and inner problems, and it is easy, and I must say quite fashionable, to blame one's angst or low self-esteem on one's parents.

Here is a checklist to help you establish whether your parents did or did not love you, and whether you may be holding a misperception.

✧ Did your parents embrace you and show any tenderness in your younger years – even if this may have fallen away in your teenage years and adulthood?

✧ Did one of your parents make any decisions about their lives that put you first? For example, did they give up a lover and stay with your other parent for your sake, or give up a job to stay at home with you (most likely a mother's situation)?

✧ Did your parents take you on holidays that were geared towards children? For example, did they take you to a holiday camp rather than to an upmarket resort that didn't have facilities for children but would have suited them better?

✧ Did your parents argue with you about your school work – insisting on homework being done before play, for instance – or did they show interest in your school?

✧ Did your parents make any sacrifice for you when it came to your education or well-being? For example, did they spend money on school uniforms, extra classes or private education? If your parents were poor, did they put your needs for food first?

If you have answered yes to any of these questions I can guarantee that at least one of your parents loved you. Of course, if I asked, 'Did they tell you that they loved you?' you might well answer no, because some people cannot express their love and put their feelings into actions rather than words. It is for you to interpret the actions of your parents and decide if they really loved you. And before you jump on the bandwagon – the route of the victim – and say that your mother or father didn't love you, just make sure.

If after reading this you realise that your parents did love you, ask yourself why you are blaming them. Look inside yourself and see why you need to blame someone. Start to heal yourself and work on your bitterness. Find out the real cause of it, and start to forgive (perhaps yourself) and to walk the spiritual path of self-healing.

If you have truly not been loved and were 'put up with' or worse, were abused by one or both of your parents, then you have a clear reason for the hurt and pain you hold inside. For your own sake, you will need to work hard on letting go of and healing your emotions. As long as you hold the pain and anger towards a parent they will continue to have the power to hurt you. As long as you are still hoping for love from one or both of your parents, you continue to be vulnerable to their actions and words.

Your aim is to get to the state where your parents can no longer hurt you either by what they say or do, or by denying you love. At the end of the day there is only one way forwards for you and this may be hard but, for your healing and release from this major issue and cause of pain in your life, you have to go down the path of forgiveness. You may believe that this is impossible and ask why should you after the things that have been done to you. This is not about justice, however; it is about you healing and moving on with your life. You will never be able to be truly happy while you hold on to bitterness.

STEPS TO FORGIVENESS

1. Express and let go of your emotions

We have already looked at forgiveness in terms of our aspirations (*see page 82*), so let's now see how we can relate it to this situation. To help you work through forgiving your parents let's first look at what this can mean in real terms.

When you forgive your parents you let the past go and accept your mother or father for who they are. You accept that they have faults, and in some cases these may be really major personality flaws, but the faults are there and may continue to be there. There is no point in wishing that your parents will change or suddenly become the loving parents of the cinema or the break-fast cereal adverts. You have had bad experiences because of your parents – that cannot be denied or changed – but this happened in the past. Even though you are still hurting from the experi-ence, for the sake of the future make the intention to let the past go.

To help with this write about all your feelings and anguish towards your parents, and what they did or did not do for you. Write down every single emotion and go through your child-hood – at this time it will be good to feel it all again, but see it as though you are viewing a video if it gets too painful. Allow your-self to grieve, to cry – let your emotions flow but know that as you are writing all this down you are finally going to let it go. Now find a suitable place and, calling in your angels and guides, ceremonially burn the writing and with it let go of the past. You may need to do this a few times.

2. Understanding

The next step is to understand your parents' actions a little better as this will help in your forgiveness. Understand them for what they are – a product of their own past experiences. You may well find that they in turn were shown little affection and love. They may well have been abused and mistreated by one or both parents. This will in itself make it difficult for them to bring love to you. They may not have had role models showing them love in their lives.

There are some cultures that have had a particularly hard time in this respect. Until quite recently in China, for example, it was very rare for parents to show love to their children. They would feed them and educate them as a matter of duty, and this legacy has been passed on to many of today's children. However, television and films are now readily available to these children, so they have had other role models and know how to show and give love. They are treating their children differently – they are breaking the cycle. For your part you also need to work on understanding your parents and finding reasons for their behaviour and attitudes. Once you have done this you will find it easier to take the next step.

3. What has this given you?

Check what character traits and understanding you have gained from having uncaring parents – they could include strength, independence, empathy for others who are unloved, compassion and so on. Take some time to write down everything that you have gained. What you have lost will have been well catalogued – I am sure you have gone over and over the list – but the positive growth and development you have made is where you need to focus now.

4. Acceptance and forgiveness

Do your best to accept your parents for what they are. Once you can live with this for a while try to find it in your heart to move to the final step of forgiving them. I have already discussed forgiveness in Chapter 4, and in this section I have included a meditation that helps you to forgive (*see page 85*).

Forgiveness is a healing for yourself and clears the way to your future happiness. By holding on to the pain inflicted by someone in the past you are allowing them to hurt you again in the present. Don't give them that power.

Before we leave this section on whether you received love from your parents, I would like to tell you about two women I know who have had difficulties with their parents and how this has affected them. The first story involves a friend of mine who I shall call Melinda. Although Melinda was brought up in London, England, her parents adhered firmly to the beliefs and attitudes of their traditional Indian Sikh culture. Like so many people of her generation, Melinda lived in two very different cultures through her schooling and her social and home lives.

When Melinda was 18 years old she met a man and fell in love. Her parents were unaware of this liaison until the day she realised that she was pregnant. The pain and suffering that they all went through was immense. Her parents were shamed beyond belief, for not only had their daughter been compromised and, in their eyes, abused, but the man was not of their faith, which compounded the enormity of the trauma for them. The full wrath of their anguish fell upon Melinda at the very time when she needed support. She felt their hatred and bitterness when she needed their love.

Melinda lost the baby and the man she loved, and during the coming years was reminded of her disgrace daily. Eventually, this drove her to leave the house and, although she was still filled with remorse, she withstood the anger and upset of her parents when they objected to her leaving home and buying her own apartment. This made her feel stronger and she threw all her attention and focus on her career, which was becoming more and more successful. After this first step away she was able to make an even greater step towards freedom by moving overseas with her job some years later.

Throughout all this time Melinda didn't meet another man who inspired her, and although she had plenty of boyfriends no great thresholds were stepped across on her path to meet the person who could share her life. Her resentment towards her parents was always immersed in her love for them, and the feeling of guilt she still carried for being the cause of so much pain and anguish for them.

Melinda came to see me when she realised that over 20 years had passed since the experience with the man in her past and she wondered why, despite forgiving him and cutting her cords to him, she was still unable to meet another person and to achieve success in her love life. It didn't take us too long to work out that in fact the problem wasn't with the man but with her parents. She still held the guilt and some measure of anger towards them for their lack of understanding of her situation and her feelings at that time. She still had an 18-year-old girl inside her who was grieving over the baby, her lost love and the rejection from her parents.

From her position of maturity Melinda was able to understand better the deep feelings of shame that had caused her parents to treat her so badly at that time. She focused upon the true cause of her problem, meditated on the situation and, with a little releasing help from me, let the pain go by healing the 18-year-old girl with love, and forgiving her parents. She immediately felt the blocks of the past lift and I know she will soon meet the man of her dreams – she is ready for a happy-ever-after ending! She will also find that her relationship with her parents – although vastly improved already – will get even better from now on.

What did this experience do for Melinda – what are its positive outcomes? She has become incredibly successful in her career and her self-esteem is extremely well balanced and positive. She has learned to stand alone without parental approval and encouragement, and she is a very strong and determined woman. She has turned every aspect of her experience around for her own good. She has lived overseas, away from her family, for some years and has developed a great circle of good friends who are supportive and loving and also great fun, so she has fully compensated for her lack of family support in her day-to-day life. She still loves her parents and can see their good and weaker points and accepts them as they are – she has learned tolerance and understanding. She has also learned the benefits of self-understanding and self-healing.

The other story I want to relate to you is even more horrific. It concerns a woman whose parents had lived through the Second World War in Europe. Her father was a Nazi sympathiser and held an extremely intolerant attitude towards physical imperfection. When my friend – let's call her Mary – was born with weak and slightly deformed legs, he wanted nothing to do with her. He turned against her and refused to have anything to do with her from then on.

When Mary was in her early teens she became very ill and the family moved to another country, leaving her behind to be nursed by a distant cousin. The father, who was a doctor, left the medication for her treatment and the money for her funeral and burial! Some time after the parents had left, the cousin became suspicious and stopped the medication. Mary's health improved immediately!

When Mary left school she trained to be a nurse – having spent so much time in hospitals due to her own condition she decided to help others. Her legs remained a great cause of pain and continue to be painful to this day, but she has learned to overcome all the obstacles that she has met in her life. She has forgiven her father and accepted him with great compassion. She is now a healer and helps others with their own emotional problems. She is a great example of living a positive and spiritual life and growing through one's adversities into a role model for us all. Like Melinda, she has healed herself through forgiveness.

DO YOU STILL SEEK THE APPROVAL OF YOUR PARENTS?

It is a natural instinct to want our parents' approval and praise. We want them to be proud of us and tell us so. We want them to back our plans and projects and give us encouragement. Unfortunately, some parents are unable to give this sort of support. They may have set ideas and dreams of a different future for you. They may so desire your future security that they see you in a profession or job that stands for success and monetary security in their minds; as a consequence, they may push you towards a career that may not suit you. You may feel rejected by them if they don't see your point of view, or if they just feel unable to give you their approval and support.

The problems continue as you get older if you still crave their support, if you still want their support and love. If they cannot give you this, don't keep pressing to receive it but look for it elsewhere in your life. If you don't, you will continue to be disappointed and feel rejected throughout your life – and constant rejection will be disastrous for your self-esteem.

Just get on with your life your way and treat your parents lovingly and respectfully, but be your own person. Make your own decisions and follow your own path. If your parents don't like your partner then keep them apart as much as possible, otherwise you will be caught in the middle of the strife. Learn the lessons that their attitudes provide you with and use them when bringing up your own children. You will be in a good position to realise that acceptance, love and praise in childhood are important factors in creating a balanced adult.

I have encountered several women who are over 40 years old and still seeking the approval of their mothers. They are repeatedly having their hearts broken by mothers who just cannot be warm and kind to their daughters – who continually criticise them and bring them down.

The constant need for approval from the daughter is an energy flow that attaches itself to the mother, creating a hook of energy. The mother feels the energy attachment and feels threatened in some way. She is also irritated by her daughter's neediness. Maybe she feels it's a responsibility – a demand that she cannot fulfil. The anger that is created by her inadequacy is then turned around against her daughter. Imagine someone continually plucking at your sleeve – that's a little how it works, only on an energetic level. The mother tries to flick off the clinging energy and does so by saying hurtful things and being sarcastic, wounding and rude.

There are many other reasons for a mother's negative attitude towards her daughter – one is jealousy. If the father has a special relationship with the daughter – which is often the case – the mother can be envious of her and this is turned into hurtful behaviour. She may also be jealous if her daughter has a better life than she herself has had, or if she is more attractive, more successful or even more confident.

CUTTING THE ENERGY HOOKS OF NEED

You may like to follow the following simple technique to cut through the energy hooks that you have created between you and your mother by your need for praise, love and approval. It has proved to work well for those who have been troubled by this problem.

✧ Find a quiet place and make yourself comfortable.

✧ Breathe in deeply four times, dropping your shoulders and relaxing the muscles in your body.

✧ Connect to your divine guidance.

✧ See yourself totally connected to the Earth by roots coming from the bottom of your feet that grow down into the centre of the Earth.

✧ Imagine yourself in a beautiful garden that is surrounded by a tall brick wall. This place is your sanctuary and private place for healing and peace.

✧ Feel the tranquillity and serenity of the beautiful garden.

✧ In the garden there is a pool, and beside the pool there is a bench – move to the bench and sit down.

✧ Visualise a fountain playing in the centre of the pool, creating ripples on the surface that spread and spread over the surface of the water.

✧ Know that the problems you have with your mother are causing ripples and affecting everyone in your family. Intend to let go of your mother. Intend to cut the ties you have to her. Determine that you will no longer care about her attitude towards you.

✧ See your mother standing in front of you now (if you cannot visualise her, then just know that she is there). See the hooks that link you to her, and see golden scissors beside you on the bench.

✧ Take the scissors and cut through the energy links.

✧ Know that you cannot now be affected by your mother.

✧ Send beams of love and light to your mother and see her surrounded by light.

✧ When you are ready leave the garden knowing you are free.

One of my clients followed this process after her mother had been particularly bitchy to her over a long period of time. Whatever she said her mother disagreed with, and she constantly criticised her. My client never received a call from her mother –

she was expected to make all the calls. The afternoon that she returned home after her session she received a call. It was her mother asking her how she was and saying that she had been thinking of her. She then told her how much she loved her and apologised for her behaviour in the past. The energy threads that we create between ourselves and others are powerful and the results of clearing them can be quite amazing.

> If your biological parents didn't create you with love remember that your soul was created from the greatest love of all

DO YOU HAVE A SMOTHER MOTHER?

You may have a problem from the opposite side of the coin – a mother who completely smothers you with her love. This smothering may take the form of continually ringing you and interfering with your life, giving you countless unwanted suggestions on how to bring up your children, handle your husband/wife or always telling you how much she is worrying about you. I must say that I find it particularly irritating when anyone keeps asking me if I am all right.

Your mother may have such an attitude because anxieties and fears dominate her life, and her constant calls to you can be a manifestation of this. If she pushes herself so much into your life it could be that there is little else in her own to distract her. Although she will be acting from love and concern, you may find it difficult to cope with her behaviour and it is likely be very annoying for your partner. You can use the above exercise again to cut the hooks, but this time see them coming from her.

I have concentrated on the mother in this example of smothering love as it tends to be a mother syndrome, but you may experience this situation with any member of your family, or even a friend who is too intrusive for comfort. By following the process of letting go you can solve the problem without hurting their feelings. If you would rather use a different approach you will have to speak up and declare your feelings in a kind and gentle way. Maybe dedicate a certain time to them each week or however often it suits you, and ask them to wait with all their news for that time. Make it a special time.

DO YOU LOVE YOUR PARENTS, AND DO YOU OWE THEM RESPECT?

One of Moses' commandments was to respect your parents – so this has been part of the Christian and Jewish spiritual ethos for some time now. In all Eastern cultures respect for parents and grandparents – in fact for age in general – is a natural way of being. Duty looms large in these cultures.

In the West we have seen this respect leave our culture. The result is old people dying alone in lonely, cold bedsits, care homes bursting at the seams with the elderly, and old people being attacked on the streets and in their homes. However, I think we have moved to a state of mind generally where we expect respect to be earned. We are less likely to worship and pay homage to any person, whether they be in this world or the next. The concept of worship and duty has been replaced by love and care.

I believe our parents are probably loved more now than they have ever been, although they may not have the homage and respect that they had in the past. I personally would hate to have duty visits from children, and I certainly don't visit my mother out of duty but rather because I love her. I know she likes to see me and I want to see her too; I want to spend time with her, and I also want to please her because I love her. This is to me by far the most natural way to be. I must say we are very lucky to have an incredibly close and loving relationship.

Unfortunately, there are people who do not have such a great relationship with their parents and find spending time with them extremely difficult. Is this your situation? Should you visit your parents out of duty? I believe you should have some consideration for them and ensure that they are not suffering, but as for spending time with them – well, you must decide for yourself.

All I can say is work it the best way you can. If you love one parent but have a problem with the other, then either accept this and bear with it, or try and see one parent without the other. My parents both had a problem with my grandfather. He was abusive to my grandmother from time to time and he had a problem with his behaviour when he had been drinking. My parents would visit annually and pray that my grandfather would be reasonable while they were there, but then he blew it big time.

One night during our annual visit my grandfather turned against my father and shouted abuse and ranted for some hours. We made a hurried departure and afterwards my parents voiced their feelings to him about his awful behaviour. For some time they didn't communicate with him at all but kept in touch with my grandmother. My mother closed the situation by saying she would forgive him but never forget what he had done, and resumed the visits for the sake of my grandmother.

You will have to decide for yourself on this matter. You do not have to love your parents deeply. You cannot force feelings that are not there to feel. Just let go of the guilt that comes with this situation and treat your parents as well as you would any other person who comes into your life, with care and understanding. Don't feel guilty that you cannot have deep feelings. Sometimes it is guilt that makes us tetchy and antagonistic towards someone, so if you can be free of guilt you will find it easier to be pleasant to them.

I personally did not love my father – he wasn't part of my life at all – but I had deep love for my stepfather. There is a dilemma that some people experience if they are adopted. When they find their biological parents they expect to feel filial love and, of course, this may not be possible because to all intents and purposes their parents are actually strangers to them. I don't hold with the saying that blood is thicker than water – in my experience deep love comes from the experience of sharing and caring.

WHAT IF YOUR PARENTS SEEM TO FAVOUR ONE OF YOUR SIBLINGS?

How do you react to one of your parents having a favourite? Does this affect you at all? I suppose most parents must have favourites but generally they try not to show their preferences. Occasionally, however, I meet someone who is really affected by a parent favouring one of their brothers or sisters. It can cause resentment and jealousy – feelings that you would rather not experience at all, but they keep coming up no matter how hard you try to mask them or deny them.

Small children can become very angry at any sign of preference or favouritism, and they stamp and yell to show their disapproval. We cannot really do this when we get older without being antisocial. However, if you have such feelings you need to do something about them. What you are working on here is good old-fashioned, green-eyed jealousy.

Letting go of jealousy

I think the key to letting go of jealousy is to work on your own self-esteem. Low self-esteem breeds the conditions for jealous attitudes. If you are fully happy with yourself you won't worry too much what people think of you or how they treat others compared with yourself. If you are content with yourself you will be big enough to let someone else, a brother or sister in this case, get more financial support or more attention than yourself. These situations are often spiritual challenges and are put there to test us. We may even have decided to experience unfair treatment in order to gain the opportunity of rising above it and strengthening ourselves emotionally and spiritually.

Turn your challenges into opportunities

HOW DO YOU FEEL WHEN A PARENT REMARRIES?

One of the major causes of jealousy with parents can occur when one of your parents remarries. It can be very difficult to adjust to a new person in your parent's life who will obviously receive a lot of attention and love. If your mother or father has remarried or taken a new partner after a divorce you may have the added complication of feeling disloyal to your other parent if you show any positive feelings to the new partner.

My best advice to you on this score is to focus entirely on the happiness of your mother or father – whoever has remarried. Anything else is selfish – after all, you are making your own life now and their happiness has to be the greatest concern for you.

You may not like their new choice – you cannot force yourself to like anyone – but if you can possibly bear with it, you will be doing a very loving and generous act for your parent. Having been in this situation myself I know how difficult it is for all concerned: the parent, the new partner and the children. It requires a great deal of tolerance to work through this, especially in the early days and especially if you share a home.

Bear in mind that the love your mother or father had for you before they met their new partner will not change. Parents do not stop loving their children just because of a change of circumstances – they may not have quite as much time to dedicate to them, but they will still love them just as much. The worse thing you can do is to start to put pressure on your parent, boycott them or tell them how little you feel for their new choice.

One of my husband's friends lost his wife after a long period of disability. He was a dedicated and caring husband all the time his wife was alive and nursed her through her many years of illness. A year after she died he announced a new liaison – actually a really lovely lady. Unfortunately, his children totally rejected her and made his life quite miserable by announcing their rejection and refusing to see her with him at any time. I personally suspected that the question of their inheritance may have had a bearing on their attitude! This poor man had to travel overseas and visit his children alone whenever he wanted to see them. I am glad to say he stuck with his choice and refused to bend to their demands that he give her up – in fact, he married her, which I thought was a great step for him to take in the circumstances. The children chose to walk a very selfish path in this case and their bitterness and self-centred attitude will only have brought them unhappiness.

If your parents divorce it is important to show support for both of them if you possibly can without getting drawn into taking sides. This is quite a challenge in some cases. You will need to surround yourself with light and hope that all the negative emotions that can appear in these situations do not land on you! When people are upset and hurt there is a tendency for them to pass on their pain as anger, and this is often directed towards their closest family.

You will need armour plating to survive a parental divorce. If you can detach yourself a little from the emotions that surround you, you will run less risk of stepping forwards and saying something that will inflame the situation and that you will later regret.

TO PROTECT YOURSELF FROM OTHER PEOPLE'S EMOTIONS

This short meditative process can help to separate you from the negative energies of the painful emotions that you may encounter if your parents separate, or in other cases where a conflict is being played out around you. You can carry out this technique at any time of the day.

✧ Find a quiet spot where you can concentrate.

✧ Close your eyes and breathe in deeply several times. This will slow down your heartbeat and calm you down.

✧ Call to the angels and your spirit guides to be with you and surround you with light. This divine light is of the very highest vibration energy and will help to keep you peaceful in chaotic and troubled atmospheres.

✧ See a beam of the light coming down from the heavens and through the top of your head. Sense that you are filled and overflowing with this loving energy.

✧ Now imagine that you are being handed a cloak of silver – wrap it around yourself and put the hood over your head so that you are totally immersed in its shining light.

✧ Now see a great, egg-shaped bubble of light and sense that you are stepping into it. This will seal your energy field – your aura – and prevent any of the negativity that surrounds you from affecting you.

✧ Put a smile on your face and go out and face the music!

Bear in mind that when people are really distressed they will be looking for things to make them more upset. Under such circumstances it is generally better to say nothing rather than to give your opinions. You will do better to send them light and just speak in a calming and unemotional manner, or wait until the heat has left the moment and speak when you are more likely to have some effect.

YOU HAVE CHOSEN A NEW PARTNER AND YOUR PARENTS DO NOT ACCEPT THEM

This is the opposite scenario. You have separated from your partner and your new choice does not have the approval of your parents. What do you do? Well, this could apply to your first, second or third choice of partner of course. But if you have divorced someone who was liked by your parents it will be harder when you turn up with your new love.

When I first introduced my husband, Tony, to my parents, they were not impressed. They did their best not to show it but, of course, I knew. They had been very fond of my first husband so it was quite natural for them to find it difficult to adjust. I appreciated their attempts to be civil and they certainly didn't say anything against Tony while I was still seeing him. Fortunately, they were completely enthralled with him when he came back into my life 15 years later and put the change of attitude down to the fact that he had changed!

What can you do if your parents are antagonistic and reject your partner? The answer is – I'm afraid – not a lot. You cannot force them to change their feelings. If you become angry about the situation you will only alienate them further. You can state your feelings and say how disappointed you are that they are not trying to accommodate your partner; that you love this person and it is your choice. You may find that over time things will change. Some people take a while to get to know others and it may take some time before they will accept a new face into the family circle. You have to play it cool, appeal to their better nature and if necessary let your partner follow his instincts – if he doesn't want to see them for a while don't press him to do so. Don't let your family spoil your relationship.

Before we leave the subject of parents I would like to spend a short time on our relationships with our brothers and sisters. Most of the issues that can come up with them will have been covered already or will be dealt with further on, when I write about relationships, but there is one particular situation that brings them into this chapter.

YOUR BROTHER OR SISTER BECOMES THE 'HEAD' OF THE FAMILY

Once the older generation of a family has passed on there is a shift in the equilibrium of the family structure. In some cases this involves a change in the power infrastructure, when one of the children takes on the role of head of the family and will now make the decisions for the entire family unit. This situation doesn't have so much impact in most family situations in the West, where we generally do not have the close family bonding that we did in the past. However, in other cultures the idea of a family head is still in place, and if the new head of a family decides to impose their attitudes and opinions on the rest of the family, this can have quite a dramatic effect on all concerned.

In my husband's family – which is of course mine too now – Tony definitely took on the role of father figure when his father died. He took on the responsibility for the welfare of his mother and to a lesser extent his siblings. He doesn't impose in any way, but they all know he is there for them if they are in trouble. There has been little discord as a result of him taking on this role, which is benevolent rather than autocratic, and the family uses our home as a base for gatherings.

Things don't always work out so well. A friend of mine has told me that her entire family has been thrown into disharmony because her second brother took over the role as head of the family when the elder brother died. He has tried to impose his views on the rest of the family and they resent it.

Sometimes we do things with good intentions and with the well-being of our families at heart, but our actions can be construed as interference and they can cause more harm than good. It is far better to show by your actions that you are there for your family if they need you and keep an open communication going, than to presume to fill a role and enforce rules. If this is to happen let it happen naturally. I guess that what I am saying is that you will earn the respect of your family more if you show them your love rather than your opinions.

I have, of course, only touched on the many situations and challenges that our parents create for us. Each of these experiences will, in some way, serve us – even if it is by helping us to empathise with others and develop our compassion. I will now move on to see how our children, stepchildren and grandchildren can affect our lives and offer perhaps the most challenging scenarios for us to work with on our day-to-day path. Those of you who do not have children can either skip the next chapter, or read it and thank your lucky stars that you have not had to face these particular hurdles!

Chapter Nine

YOU AND CHILDREN, STEPCHILDREN AND GRANDCHILDREN

I n this chapter we look at issues that can occur with you and your children and grandchildren and see if we can find help with these challenges through spiritual guidance. As you become more at ease with yourself the ripple effect will definitely help your child – from the time your baby is in your womb until you pass on there is a very special bond between you and your child, so naturally they will be tremendously affected by your inner state. As you gain inner happiness and peace, you will find that they will reflect this through their behaviour.

A mother automatically connects to all aspects of love when her baby is born. Gentleness, tenderness, caring and generosity all flow in abundance, but as you encounter some of the challenges you face as a parent, you need to draw on all your spiritual aspirations – particularly patience and tolerance.

Children bring the greatest blessings and the greatest pain. They challenge our capacity for fear and develop our capacity to love.

SHALL WE HAVE A CHILD?

Let's start with a question that a lot of couples are now facing – a question that would not have been asked a hundred years ago. In the past the main spiritual motivation for marriage was to procreate – to receive as many children as God gave you. The world has moved on and if all still held this belief the already depleted earthly resources would be completely exhausted. We therefore need to be careful about the numbers of children we bring into the world.

The cycle of life belief is that we make a decision before we are born about our parents, the location of our birth and our life plan. Our character and the circumstances of our life will also be greatly affected by the planetary forces while we are on Earth. These will help to create the challenges that we wish to overcome and assist us with the achievements we wish to experience.

The positioning of the planets affects the energies that prevail on Earth at any time. We are particularly influenced by the compilation of the planetary forces at the moment we are born – the moment when our soul and physical body become as one for this lifetime's journey on Earth. Anyone who has had a full astrological reading will know how uncannily correct the readings based on accurate birth data can be.

Let me just interject at this point with my experience of birth dates and charts: it may help explain my point here. I have an Indian friend who lives in Malaysia. From time to time she visits a group of astrologers in India, and she asked me if I would be interested in having a reading. She explained how these very special 'wise men' worked. They have a copy of the records of every single soul that has and will live on Earth! They have full notes on everything that has happened to us in all our visits to Earth and on what our future visits have in store – and, of course, a detailed list of our experiences in this lifetime. These notes are called the Akashic Records and are held in the consciousness of the planet. Some years ago Indian psychics actually wrote down the notes on tablets. They are therefore accessible to us all, and not just to those gifted psychics who can read the future by accessing these records in the astral dimensions.

My friend gave these men my birth date, location of birth and full name. She also took with her information on my mother and husband for verification. They looked me up and then told her they were confused. They had found an Anne Jones who was born in England on 24 December 1945, but the husband situation was a concern. In my records, they found two husbands with the name Tony – my friend had no idea why this was (namely, because both my previous husband and my current one were called Tony). They said that my current husband was Tony Jones, but that there was another Tony – Tony Frost – in my records. When they found that my mother's details tied in with mine, they accepted that they had the right Anne Jones. Of course, I was able to verify this for my friend when she returned.

Everything the men told me about my past was absolutely correct, and they predicted things about my future that seemed very plausible. They told my friend something that I had already discovered – that our will power (our ability to make our own choices) can allow us to change the plan that we made before we were born. We can make amendments as we pass through life, and that is why some predictions can be changed. There are possibilities, probabilities and certainties. These are like windows of opportunity that we can take or reject, depending on what we feel at the time. So there may be a number of dates that would suit our life plan, but some will be better than others. We depend upon our parents to help us to get that plan off to a good start by getting our birth time right.

Your child will therefore depend partly upon you to get their birth time right – I say partly because there are many forces helping this situation. The more closely you work to your feelings and intuition, the more likely it will be that everything will be at its best.

> If you are making a decision about having a baby trust your instincts and don't just rely on logic – make the choice by feelings

As when you make all major decisions in your life, pray for help and ask to be guided to making the right choice for the highest good of all concerned. Your prayer will be answered, although you may find that the choice is not the one you were expecting.

Dealing with infertility

Tony and I were very keen to have a baby and we tried to conceive for a couple of years when we were first married. I decided in the end to trust to God and let my own desires surrender to fate. I didn't have a child and I can see now in retrospect that this was for the best, although my charts had indicated that I might have two children. I have been involved in the lives of two teenagers – my stepchildren – so maybe that counts!

Over time I have attempted to help a number of women who were desperate to conceive and were having difficulties. There are times when our fears can affect our fertility and ability to conceive a child. These fears can come from experiences in this lifetime, such as seeing a mother overwhelmed by either child-birth or parenting; or they may originate in a past-life experience. Clearing away the negative energies associated with having a child can be helpful.

MEDITATION FOR FERTILITY

This meditation will help you to release anything from your past that may be blocking you, and to share your intention to conceive with the universe and all your hidden help in the wings!

✧ Find a quiet and relaxing place to sit.

✧ Breathe in deeply four or five times and let your body go soft – drop your shoulders. Just sit quietly for a few moments.

✧ See your roots going down into the ground beneath you. Feel a strong connection to the Earth.

✧ Call in your guides and angels to help you and say any prayer that feels good for you at this time. If you wish, connect to a spiritual Master who is associated with fertility and children, for example Mother Mary or Kwan Yin.

✧ See yourself in a beautiful garden. This is your inner haven of healing. It is tranquil and serene, and you can relax in it and release your fears.

✧ Say out loud, 'I let go of all aspects of my past that are preventing me from conceiving a child.'

✧ Cup your hands and see balls of colour emerging into your hands – these represent the fears from your past. Throw the balls into the air and see them float off to the sun, where they trans-form into light. Know that you have let these fears go for ever.

✧ Breathe in deeply and reinforce the releasing of these fears with your out-breath as you breathe out forcibly. Imagine you are blowing away all negativity.

✧ Now say, 'I release all vows and commitments that no longer serve me.'

✧ Again breathe out forcibly.

✧ See a golden egg in your hands. Hold it to your heart and feel it merge into your heart centre – in the centre of your chest. Feel love flowing through you and around you.

✧ Trust that whatever is for your highest good will arise.

✧ Step back into the room.

Do whatever you can to ensure the conception you require – if necessary have the medical checks and treatment that are available to you and then let the outcome go. You can make yourself incredibly miserable by constantly yearning for something you do not have. Believe that what is right for you will occur.

Abortion

You are pregnant and for whatever reason you do not want to have the baby, so you are considering an abortion. This is a very controversial subject but I would reiterate at this point the ethos of personal spirituality – we make our own decisions and take full responsibility for ourselves. There is no cut and dried edict, no law cast in stone on this subject.

No expectant mother makes the decision to terminate her baby lightly, and much pain and anguish go into choosing whether to proceed or not. However, let me just tell you what I have learned about the arrival of the soul in the foetus; it may help you a little. It is very rare for the soul to join the foetus at the time of conception for a permanent stay. It may and most likely will visit for a short time, and then return to the astral planes while the physical form grows in its early weeks.

I used to have a Monday morning energy-healing session, which was open to anyone who wanted to come along to give and receive healing. One of my regular visitors was an expectant mother. One day as we stood with our hands on her stomach sending love through to the baby, I suddenly became aware of a presence in the room and then felt it move into the baby. It was the baby's soul arriving. We all felt the light and the loving energy. The woman was about five months pregnant at the time.

On another occasion, a friend of mine was giving birth when I arrived in Hong Kong for a visit. Another friend and I went straight to the hospital and sent light to the mother and baby as the baby was being born. The father came out to see us soon afterwards and declared that he had seen the baby's soul arrive just at the time when the baby emerged from its mother.

A baby's soul can arrive at any time, but it is very rarely with its new body until quite some time into its development. You do not kill a soul when you abort a foetus – although you do take away an opportunity for its life. If you abort or miscarry there is a high possibility that the soul will wait for the next opportunity to come into this world.

Recently, two of my friends have been through a very difficult time. They have been warned by their doctors that their babies could be suffering from Down's syndrome, which causes a baby to be born with a brain disorder. If there is a possibility that a baby may have Down's syndrome, doctors recommend an amniocentesis test. The problem is that this test has caused miscarriages in some women. This puts the parents into a dilemma about whether they should or should not have the test. One of my friends decided to have the test because for her the fear of the unknown was worse than having the test; the other decided not to have it. In both cases, the decisions were made after meditation and prayer. Both women eventually gave birth to normal children.

If you are faced with this type of dilemma remember that you are not alone, and if you surrender to the highest good the outcome will be as it should be. In the cases I've just discussed, both sets of parents had decided that they would have the child even if they knew that it had a problem; they knew they would love their child no matter what. That was their choice – you may feel differently.

A BABY'S WELL-BEING
IN THE WOMB

While you are carrying a baby it is important to stick to a regime of self-discipline. This applies to expectant fathers as well as to mothers. You will already know of the harm that smoking and excessive drinking will do to your baby. You will also be aware that the food you eat will be nurturing the foetus, and that it is therefore doubly important to eat fresh fruits and vegetables, and to choose organic and natural food without additives where possible.

What you may not be aware of is the effect on your baby of your own emotions. You may not be able to keep your emotions under wraps, but if you meditate daily and keep yourself as peaceful as you possibly can, you will be giving your baby the very best start in life. Past-life therapy can take a person back to a past life via their early days and time in the womb. I have frequently heard people who have regressed to this stage say how disturbed they are or worried about their mother because she is so sad or angry.

In some cases a baby can sense if it is unwanted and the rejection can stay with them until later life. A baby can also tell if its father – if he is sharing life with the mother – is emotional in any way. When I regressed to the womb I picked up a great sadness and distress in my mother. This came from the fact that she had fallen out with my father and was in love with another man. Of course, we cannot always dictate the events that occur while we are pregnant, but both the mother and father need to be aware that any disagreements and discord between them will affect the baby.

Birth timing

Bearing in mind all the outside forces that can affect our arrival, from contraception and abortion to miscarriage, it is nothing short of a miracle that we get here at all. Our arrival time can also be affected by, for example, doctors who want the weekend off and decide that an induction would be a good idea.

I personally think we should allow a baby to arrive at the time that it wants to appear, and I would fight tooth and nail to allow a birth to be as natural as possible, with minimal interference from doctors and nurses. Of course, both the mother's and the baby's health must be priorities. However, you shouldn't fret and worry about these issues too much as the forces of the universe, the guidance of our spirit guides and our own intuition all contrive to bring a new soul into the world at the right time.

Also don't worry too much about whether your delay in having a baby will affect the journey of another soul – your baby's. I believe that if you are to have an influence on someone's life, their soul will find a way to be born into your family or to a close friend anyway. You may well find that you feel particularly close to a niece or nephew, or to a godchild – this could be because you have a close soul connection with them and are to help them either in their infancy or when they are older.

THE PROBLEMS FACING A WORKING MOTHER

Is it OK to go back to work once you have had your baby? This is another tricky question. Those of you who are in a desperate financial state will not have a choice. If the man of the house is out of work there is a good case for the woman to work and the man to be at home and be a housefather. I have seen this work very well and it has been the choice of several people I know, not necessarily because of the financial aspect, but because the woman has a powerful career or vocation that she wants to fulfil. Of course, this only works if the man is quite happy to be at home.

A baby needs constant attention – feeding, changing and nursing, but most importantly a consistent flow of love. It is best if this is provided by the mother, father or grandmother. A stranger who takes care of the baby as a minder will not necessarily have the same love bonding with the baby, and this is something you need to bear in mind when making choices in this area. If you can afford a live-in nanny you will at least be able to provide continuity for the baby; many crèches have a number of staff and the constant changes of smell and the feel of different people can be too disruptive for a small baby.

To my mind the most important job in the world is that of a mother, followed by that of a father. I say this because the majority of people who come to me with problems have issues that go back to their childhood. These issues include abandonment, lack of security and low self-esteem stemming from a lack of demonstrated love as a child.

I occasionally see people who have had wonderfully loving and stable childhoods, with balanced and loving parents who stayed together, created a proper family home, and gave their children full support and plenty of loving attention. These people generally have grown up to be balanced and effective adults. Therefore to my mind the role of mother has to be of key importance. If everyone had a loving childhood there would be fewer wars, less hatred and a smaller number of emotionally damaged adults in the world.

If you are thinking about going back to work after having a child, check your reasons carefully.

✧ THE EXTRA MONEY WOULD BE USEFUL – Is it actually more important than being there for your child? Bear in mind if you are working to pay for toys, games and clothes for your children, that in the long run they will remember your love but forget the toys.

✧ YOU NEED TO FULFIL YOURSELF – Is there no other way other that you can do this other than being employed full time? What about taking an evening class to learn a new skill? How about some voluntary work that has flexible hours? How about starting a creative pastime?

✧ THE FAMILY CANNOT MANAGE FINANCIALLY WITHOUT A SECOND WAGE – Can you find an employer who allows flexi-hours, or work from home so that you can spare some hours in the day for your baby? If you have to go back to work, is there any chance that you can leave it until your child is five and at school all day?

If you do decide to work full-time, you will need to cope with the guilt issue. Once you have chosen to work, leave the guilt behind. Guilt brings pressures and stress that will make you less fun to be with at home and put added pressure on your family relation-ships, and it will prevent you from being fully operational at work. Guilt will deplete your energy, so put it behind you with the knowledge that it is better for your family to have a happy and fulfilled mother part-time, than a bitter and resentful one full-time.

> A harmonious home and demonstrable love are the greatest gifts you can give a child

YOUR CHILDREN ARGUE A LOT – SHOULD YOU INTERFERE?

It is difficult to know how much you should interfere in arguments between children, whether they be disputes between your own children or their confrontations with other youngsters. Sibling rivalry can dominate the early years, and it can be quite a noisy preoccupation! You can suggest moderation in the way your children express their anger, so that they let it out, but do so as harmlessly as possible. Bear in mind that suppression of the emotions is an adult problem, and children shouldn't have to worry too much about it. Concentrate on the expression of the anger rather than the anger itself.

The very best way to help children is to provide them with boundaries beyond which you are not prepared to go, or to let them go. Consistency seems to be the name of the game. It can involve repetitive observations on the right way to behave towards and treat other people – teaching sharing and consideration for the feelings and possessions of others – and consistent emphasis on what you are prepared to tolerate in the expression of any emotions that may come up during play.

PROVIDING A ROLE MODEL

Children copy what they see and hear so work on providing them with a role model for the best way to socialise by the way you and your partner act not only towards each other and them, but also towards outsiders. I find it most distressing to hear a mother shouting and screaming at her child in order to enforce the fact she wants them to be quiet. How can this work? I'm not sure that debating situations with a two-year-old is the most effective way either. On that point you will have to follow your own intuition, but remember that you have a right to some peace and harmony in your home, and if a child is in danger of taking over with its emotional tantrums you need to have your say.

MEDITATION

Why not include your children in your meditation sessions? All the children I know love to meditate – especially if you use guided meditations – as they have a natural ability to use their imaginations and don't have the inhibitions that adults develop. Meditation helps children to settle down before sleep; if they are encouraged to focus on children around the world who are suffering or deprived, it also teaches them to develop their love and compassion. You can show them how to give some of their time and attention to other people with distance healing. Children also love angels and it is a great idea to encourage them to talk to their guardian angel.

MEDITATION FOR CHILDREN

- ✧ Turn off the phones and find a quiet space – it can be your child's bedroom.

- ✧ Make sure you are sitting comfortably.

- ✧ Breathe in slowly and deeply four times.

- ✧ Call in the angels: see them standing around the bed. They are here to protect you while you sleep. Thank the angels for being here.

- ✧ Call your very special angel to stand at the foot of the bed.

- ✧ Imagine that you are surrounded by a beautiful pink light – this is the angels sending you their love.

✧ Take the pink light into your hands and hold it to you – feel it filling you up right to the top.

✧ Now imagine that between your hands there are lots of tiny children – these are all the children in the world who are sad, sick, hungry and frightened, and who need lots of love.

✧ See the pink light go from your hands and fill the children; see them smiling, happy and well.

✧ See any children you know need help filled with the lovely pink love light.

✧ Thank your angels and ask them to stay with you throughout the night.

HEALING

I have found that if healing is given to pregnant mothers the results are less traumatic birthing followed by quiet and peaceful babies. I haven't done a full study on this but have found that all the mothers who have received hands-on energy healing have been delighted with the results and said their babies definitely benefited from it.

Small children love healing. My granddaughter would come to me whenever she hurt herself for a touch of my magic, and her aches and pains disappeared almost instantly; healing works very well if applied just after the event. Hands-on healing is also a very natural method of healing – after all, mothers have put their hands on their children's aches and pains for centuries.

PAST RECALLS
FROM CHILDREN

Up to the age of four or five, when they go to school, children often have memories of their past life or lives. Many parents ridicule their children for these 'imaginations', and this is hard for the child as the recalls are real and often very vivid.

My friend Brenda remembers her brother tugging his mother's arm when they were walking near their house in north London just after the war, and saying, 'Let's go to my other mother – I want to go and see the cat.' Brenda's mother became increasingly irritated with him as this went on day after day. He was forever trying to get them to go and see the house and continuously talked of his other mother. Some years later they discovered that there had been a house there, which had been bombed, and the entire family had been killed. Brenda said that her brother had been very distressed by both the dismissal of his knowledge and memory, and also the anger that his mother showed towards him because of his 'made-up stories'. Another friend of mine says that her grandchildren are always talking about their past lives and her daughter actively encourages them to do so – explaining to them what these memories are and why they have them.

Once children go to school they find so many other exciting things to grab their attention that this habit of looking back naturally fades. So don't dismiss your children's imagination and their natural intuition as it will most likely be serving them better than your own!

FOOD

The food you give your children will be the basis of their taste for life. If you bring them up on good fresh fruits and vegetables, and a minimal amount of processed and additive-free foods, you will be giving them a great start.

Food additives are one of the main causes of hyperactivity in children and can aggravate Attention Deficiency Disorder (ADD) syndrome and Attention Deficiency with Hyperactivity Disorder (ADHD). Also watch out for sugar. If your children are prone to mood swings and unprovoked emotional outbursts, make sure that they don't go too long between meals, as they may well have a low blood sugar level. This, of course, is not treated with a bar of chocolate!

Should you encourage your children to be vegetarian? I am a little wary of suggesting children should be vegetarian as it may be difficult for a mother to understand how to handle a totally balanced vegetarian diet, but I would say that children should not eat too much red meat and eat more fish. Encouraging your children to eat fresh fruits instead of processed sugar is also good for them. I have a friend whose children think that an apple is the ideal snack between meals – this is great conditioning.

SCHOOLS

This is where personal preference must be paramount. Do you believe in and can you afford private schooling? Is it morally right to give your children a 'leg-up' by sending them to private school? I don't think it is morally wrong, but unfortunately the growing number of private schools is creating a bigger divide between the haves and have nots. A local school is fine in many cases, but standards do vary and it also depends on the character of the child.

I went to a small local junior school in the middle of Wandsworth in London, followed by a comprehensive school, and got a reasonable education. I have never felt that my education has held me back from anything that I have set myself to do. Even the best schools in the world cannot teach the determination to succeed, the ability to mix well, the temperament to get the best from life, a positive attitude towards life and a happy disposition. Add a heavy dose of love for humanity and all animals, supportive and loving parents, and an understanding of the balance between mind, body and soul, and you have the recipe that I believe goes a long way to making a happy individual.

What if the local school is really bad? One of the reasons why my husband bought a house in Buckingham was that the local grammar school was considered to be one of the best in the country and definitely in the radius of his workplace at Aylesbury. That may seem a drastic reason for choosing where to live. But is it? We move homes to be near our selected workplace, so why not to be near to a good school? There is nothing 'unspiritual' in wanting the best for your children.

If you want to send your children to a private school and can afford to do so, you may also like to send some money to support education in a Third World country. There are some wonderful charity schemes that will allow you to help a child have a basic education where otherwise it would have none.

As I have lived as an expatriate for a number of years I have come across a number of issues surrounding boarding schools. I know all the reasons why boarding schools are a good idea when families move countries every few years – disruptive schooling can result in poor exam results, poor local schools, difficulties in keeping friends and so on. However, the pain and upset to both parents and children when children have to live away from their families is immense. Generally speaking, there is no substitute for a happy home that can nurture the continued emotional growth of a child. Yes, boarding schools do encourage self-reliance and self-discipline, but I'm not convinced about them. Unfortunately, children often suppress their true feelings about this issue just to please their parents, so it may not be until much later that the effects will be known.

One of my friends has a boyfriend who was brought up in Kenya and was sent away to school at the age of five. He still finds it difficult to have a close relationship and some of the attitudes that make him a bit of a loner go back to that time. Sending a child away, especially if they are under the age of eleven, will nearly always be perceived as abandonment by the child either then or in later life. Use your intuition and your knowledge of your child; some children adapt to boarding school better than others.

TEENAGE WOES, HORMONES OR REBELLION?

Without doubt the hardest time in bringing up children comes when they reach puberty. From the age of eleven you can be faced with irrational behaviour, mood swings, 'parent hating', petulance, rebellion, and loss of self-esteem and confidence. The teenage woes disturb households all over the world once the hormones kick in and a child begins its struggle to emerge from the chrysalis of childhood into the frightening, overwhelming, exciting and challenging world of adulthood.

What can you do when your well-behaved and obedient child becomes this moody, negative, uncooperative individual who seems intent on going against your wishes and advice? You may at times feel you have spawned a monster! That charming young boy who couldn't do enough to please his mother suddenly leaves behind him a trail of empty mugs everywhere from the bathroom to under the bed, has a sudden aversion to washing, wears the most inappropriate clothes, has a hairstyle based on his current football idol, and generally becomes as morose as Gollum. *You can do nothing!* You just have to sit it out as patiently as you can – living with a teenager is, after all, a lesson to you in patience and tolerance!

Eventually, your monster will undergo an amazing transformation and the duckling will turn into a swan. The most important thing to remember is that it is only a transition stage

– although it may seem to be a long one – and that you need to keep the door open for your child no matter what they do in those difficult years. Send light and healing to them regularly. Understand that you can only be responsible for yourself – you cannot learn the lessons for your sons and daughters, or go through the growing pains for them. Each of us has to go through this process for ourselves as we become adults.

Remember that your child's rejection of you is not a personal rejection; it is an outwards projection of the confusion your child is facing within them as their bodies change and become sexually alive and their perception of life shifts. It could be that you are being rejected as your child's ideas of life from infancy are rejected. If you have shared as much wisdom and good advice with your child in the earlier years as you can, and have been a good role model for them, sooner or later all will be well. Make sure you leave the door open – you will only have regrets if you fall out and go through the 'never darken my door again' syndrome. I promise you that it does get better!

ACCEPTING YOUR CHILDREN AS THEY ARE

We have an expression in our family: 'I accept you as you are, warts and all.' As it happens, there are no knobbles on the faces of our family, but this is a statement of total acceptance. No one is perfect, no one can meet all the expectations of another, and this goes for children as well as adults. Much angst is created in families when parents decide on a blueprint that they imagine their children will fit. Remember that your child has not only your genes creating their individuality, but their own soul energy as well.

The fusion of a soul and a foetus, with its genetic inheritance, results in the creation of a unique being who is set on a deter-mined path on Earth. Your child will have an innate knowledge of what they need to do and where their path will take them. Apart from guiding the child away from obvious dangers such as unprotected sex, drugs and excesses that damage health, why not let your teenager determine the path that they are to tread? This may take them off into the wilderness for a while – but maybe they need to face the challenge of self-determination and to learn lessons by experience, even if it is the hard way.

Bear with your child if they tell you they need to travel, live overseas, be an artist or join a commune, or if they ask you to acknowledge that they are gay. Your support and love will help them to make difficult decisions more easily, and they will be less likely to follow a path of rebellion if you do not impose any dictatorial and dominating views on them. We all have a tendency to push against any opposition, and teenagers do this as an art form.

FATHERS AND SONS

I have noticed over and over again how difficult it is for a father and son to have a truly close and trusting relationship. I have seen men who I find open and easy-going become stilted and prickly when their father is around. I know men who are outgoing and expansive normally to clam up and become terse and uncommunicative when in the company of a son.

I believe the basis of many of these difficulties is the need of the son to please the father and the expectations and hopes that men have for their sons. I have heard sons say so often, 'Whatever I do I cannot please him,' and fathers say equally often, 'I just cannot seem to talk to my son; he won't let me come close to him.'

While a boy is growing up his greatest idol and role model is his father. Up to a certain age a father can do no wrong in the eyes of a boy – he is his hero. You see small boys trying to walk and sit like their father, trying to emulate him in everything they do and watching him avidly. So often, though, fathers will lose touch with the world and reality that their son is inhabiting.

If you criticise the world that your son lives in he will believe you are criticising him. This can apply to your criticism of anything from computer games to the language of the young. Boys have a very tender pride and if they feel that they are being put down by their hero, they start to become introverted and hold back their feelings. The closest relationships seem to be created when a father takes a genuine interest in the reality of the son and puts out few demands or expectations of how he should be or where he should go as he becomes a young man, and when the son accepts that his father has faults like other humans and allows tolerance to keep the doors of communication and love open.

SELF-RESPONSIBILITY AND SOCIAL AWARENESS

I suppose one of the greatest lessons you can teach a child is how to be self-responsible and independent. We could say that parenthood is the responsibility to lead your children towards being as good as they can be, to reach the heights that they can reach and to help them become adults who can be happy, peaceful and contented. I am sure there are many more attributes for living that can be added to this list, but there is one in particular that I think should be regarded as an aim. This is to be socially responsible and aware. It involves realising that we do not live in a cocoon and that the needs and problems of others – no matter where they are in the world – should be high in our consciousness, and that we should help them when and where we can.

STEPCHILDREN

Before I leave the subject of children I must talk briefly about stepchildren. Because there are so many broken partnerships it is quite normal for children to be brought up at least partially by people who are not blood relations. All the guidelines, both practical and spiritual, that I have already covered for your own children apply equally to stepchildren. However, from experience I feel that things can be more difficult when you are a step-parent rather than a natural parent.

There are many issues that can arise. I must write here for the benefit of my own stepchildren that not all of them were problems for us, but they are issues that have been raised by many of my patients and have caused problems for them and the children. I was very lucky and, although I wouldn't go so far as to say that we had an entirely easy ride, and there were definitely defining moments, we generally managed our way through the pitfalls quite well.

Overcoming distrust and jealousy

When you join an existing family as a step-parent, or take on the role of one in a partnership with a parent, you will almost certainly face hostility of some kind. You may be stepping into the footprints of a loved mother or father lost either through divorce or death. The children will see you as an intruder; they will think you are trying to replace the missing parent and will resent you for this.

If you accept that this will happen, your expectations will not be too high, especially of the early days. It will take time for your relationship with your stepchildren to develop – it is likely that it will be years before it becomes truly strong, if it ever does. The children may never feel warmth towards you. Try not to judge them too harshly while they are making their adjustments – they will throw tantrums, have sulks, deliberately be disruptive, or withdraw – depending on their age and temperament. There may even be a battle of wills, and don't be surprised if they lie about you to either your partner or the other parent. Expect this and have broad shoulders.

Dealing with deliberate attempts to forge a rift between you and your partner

One of the usual patterns is for the child to try and come between you and your partner – this is especially relevant to girls whose father has taken a new partner. Girls and fathers have a very special relationship. It can be very close and tender, and the girl may see you getting the affection that was, in her mind, reserved for her before, particularly if her parents were not close to each other for some time before their separation. Whatever you do, don't try and make a competition out of it. Do what you can to keep the peace, and although you should express your feelings try to do it in as gentle and caring a way as possible.

Handling the relationship with the other parent

Although you may find that you have all sorts of emotions when dealing with the other parent, this is really a time to keep them to yourself. If you start to run down, argue with or in any way put down the other parent, you will make things very difficult for the children who love them. I think there is nothing worse for children than to hear one of their beloved parents being criticised and spoken of disrespectfully. I see people who at 50 years plus still have a real dislike of their step-parents because of their criticism of a natural parent. Keep your feelings to yourself, or at least say nothing in front of the children, and encourage your partner to do the same.

When it comes to stepchildren my advice is to give as much love and attention as you can and expect little in return. Then you won't be disappointed; you may be pleasantly surprised that as time goes by you discover a beautiful and lasting relationship, as I did. One of the great advantages you have with step-relationships is that expectations are far lower from them than from other relationships, so everything good that comes out of them is a wonderful bonus. Conversely, we expect a great deal from our natural parents and children, and what we actually get from them is sometimes a disappointment.

> If we take the expectations out of all our relationships, any love we get will be a wonderful surprise

As we leave the subject of how to bring up children with spiritual awareness, here is a quick summary of what has been covered in this chapter.

✧ Consistent boundaries make a child feel 'at home' and on safe ground. They ensure that a child knows what is OK for them and what will harm them or cause stress to everyone around them.

✧ Changing your views and expectations will confuse a child.

✧ You cannot love a child too much but you can over-indulge them with material things and the wrong food.

✧ Act as a role model for good spiritual attitudes and practices, such as compassion, sharing and tolerance.

✧ Encourage your child to connect with angels and understand their spiritual aspect.

✧ Show your child how to meditate and have a short meditation after their bedtime story.

◇ Avoid giving your child processed foods, sugar, cakes, crisps and so on. Give them a balanced diet of fresh organic fruits, vegetables and fish.

◇ Allow your child to develop their intuition and understand their feelings.

◇ Help your child to develop their own self-worth by encouraging them to do things for themselves and praising their efforts.

◇ Encourage your child to believe in themselves and help them step through limitations rather than discouraging them. Let them have great horizons in their dreams of the life they can achieve.

◇ Teach your child the value of commitment and loyalty.

◇ Show your child social awareness and responsibility towards the community, the nation and the world.

GRANDCHILDREN

Everyone who has a grandchild will tell you that theirs is a very special relationship, without the worries, concerns and responsibilities of parenthood. You also deal with the child from an older and wiser perspective than a parent does. You dote on your grandchildren and they love it! There is little else to say.

There is just one aspect of being a grandparent that I would like to raise and that is what to do if you know that your child is mistreating or neglecting your grandchildren. I hope you do not have to face such a situation, but if you do maybe this story will help you. If nothing else I think it highlights the absolute and all-encompassing love that grandparents can have for their grandchildren.

A lady came to see me with a long-standing problem. She was suffering from deep sadness and loss and asked if I could help her. Some years earlier she had been placed in a difficult dilemma. She discovered that her son was mistreating her young grandson. She didn't give me the full details, but the mistreatment included physical, emotional and mental abuse. Her son was a drug addict, and this naturally pleasant and loving man had become violent towards his children, especially his son.

My client realised that she had to do something and do it quickly before the child was seriously hurt. She wanted to take the child herself, but her son refused to let him go. So she informed social services of the situation. This resulted in the children being taken into care. Because of the continuing threat from the father she couldn't adopt the children herself and they were eventually adopted by a loving couple who still have the children in their care. Their grandmother was absolutely heartbroken because she knew that she would never see her grandchildren again – her only consolation was that she had done the right thing for her grandson.

What a sacrifice and what great love this lady displayed!

Chapter Ten

HAVING A LOVING
RELATIONSHIP

I n this chapter we look at the challenges that our relationships with others bring us, and how we can be spiritual in
the manner that we treat those who are close to us. A good
partnership can be a great source of comfort and support both
when there is a crisis in your life, and when you need help in
coping with your everyday pressures. How we treat our partner
and how we allow ourselves to be treated are the main themes of
this chapter.

A partnership brings up many issues for us. These include self-
esteem – not allowing yourself to be a doormat; speaking your
feelings; tolerance – allowing differences; love – showing and
receiving tenderness and respect; self-responsibility – not being
the victim and acknowledging that you co-create the situations
that arise in a relationship. Let's see how you can use your spiritual beliefs and aspirations to create the best relationship for
your mutual good.

WHAT IS THE FORMULA FOR A SUCCESSFUL AND REWARDING RELATIONSHIP?

Or is there one? Every couple has to work out their own personal format for living. I suggest you just spend a few moments focusing on your relationships and consider two questions.

✧ What are you expecting from this relationship?

✧ What do you consider to be the important guidelines for a relationship?

Write down the answers and ask your partner to do the same, then compare lists. If you are moving into a new relationship, this will highlight any differences to which you will need to pay extra attention.

Here are some guidelines for a successful relationship.

Be accepting and tolerant

Trying to get someone to change their habits and behaviour is a young person's dream – as you get older you realise that it is a pointless exercise. Learn to adapt around and live with the person as they are. This also means that you need to let your partner have time to themselves, and to allow (and in fact encourage) them to follow their own pursuits and interests. You should certainly not attempt to get them to give up the aspects of their life that don't include you.

On your part, too, ensure that you continue to do the things that make you happy whether it be visiting the gym, yoga or skydiving; be yourself – after all it was the complete package that your partner first fell in love with. We can't just select the bits we like – partnerships are not cherry-picking exercises. We cannot make our partner fit our blueprint of the ideal man or woman.

Practise tolerance – enjoy the differences

If you cannot accept the person as they are – if, for instance, they have developed hurtful attitudes that you just cannot accept – there is only one solution, and that is to leave.

If you are a woman, what do you do when your partner doesn't help you out with the home chores? Well, I can tell you what not to do – don't shout at him and nag him. It doesn't work and just creates nasty scenes. Don't waste your time. If you are a man, on the other hand, you may have your own vision of a New Woman – one who can be a working wife, mother and companion. You may, however, find that your partner would rather be a home mother and that she is reluctant to return to work after having had children. Let her be the person she wants to be – you will then have a happy partner.

Don't fight

Your partnership is not a power game or a matter of control – it's a couple of people making choices about the life they share. You know I believe in voicing your feelings so this is not about being submissive – it is about looking at things in different ways. Is it worth the argument? Is it really that important to you that you get your way? Are you doing it to show power, revenge, to get attention? Check your intentions. If you find that your opinions and choices differ tremendously, ask yourself if you really like each other and want to be together. I know that it is said that opposites attract, but like attracts like too, and is a far more harmonious option. Especially don't fight in front of the children.

Positively support each other

One of the great joys of a close partnership is that you can give each other support, particularly when you are facing challenges. You wouldn't always believe this when you see the way some people act towards each other. You may wonder if 'partnership' is actually another word for battle.

Every chance you get make an effort to show your partner support in every way you can. Rather than try to put them down, praise them, try to uplift them and make them feel better about themselves. Avoid using the 'guilt trick' – making a person feel guilty by being a victim, for example by saying, 'If you really loved me you would have remembered my mother's birthday.' It is easy to make a person feel guilty, but not very constructive to do so if you want a happy relationship. Avoid scoring points off each other. See yourselves as a unit that stands together.

> Your life together is not a battle – you will not find happiness in the victories won against each other

Demonstrate your love with words and actions

I think it is so very, very important to demonstrate the love you feel for each other. (This of course applies to your other relationships within your family too.) Little acts of kindness show your love and create a wonderful atmosphere, which allows your relationship to flourish. Say the words too – this is so important, especially if one of you is a little insecure. There isn't a woman in the world who doesn't appreciate a small gift from time to time – giving flowers is a particularly beautiful way of showing your love. Men appreciate loving words too, or the touch – not just in bed – that shows your warmth and tenderness, and those little gifts of thoughtfulness, like letting him watch his favourite television programme on Saturday night, even if it is football!

Talk to each other

When we have things on our minds we sometimes keep them inside of us while we ponder on them. To those around us, it can seem as though we are distancing ourselves, and in some cases our quietness comes across as moodiness. Excluding a partner in this way can result in tension between you and a further distancing.

Lack of communication is a common problem in relationships, and it is the easiest to put right. You may find it easier to talk about your problems and feelings when you are out of your normal environment. We often get caught up in our daily habits and routines in the home; the television can come on and talk will cease. It is a good idea to go out for a drink or a meal once a week and use that as an opportunity to air all your inner thoughts, problems and feelings. This will stop molehills from becoming mountains that can be hard to bring down. Share your dreams and hopes for the future too – this way you can be sure that you are both steering the boat in the same direction.

See your relationship as an equal partnership

Relationships often fail if you look for something in a partner that will compensate for a lack in yourself. It makes you needy and therefore vulnerable. If you go into a relationship as an equal and with the idea of sharing time and experiences together, rather than looking for what you can get out of it, you will have a far greater chance of success. Needy people with a great deal of emotional baggage from past experiences can bring burdens into a relationship.

If you meet someone with lots of healing to do make sure you are aware of it and also be realistic – it may take them some time to heal, even with your love and care. You will become involved with this person's traumas and healing process, and will be helping them to go through this. Be sure you want to take on this task. To a certain extent, we all bring some emotional scars and past hurts to a partnership, and a loving relationship is a great healer. However, very needy people can be a huge drain on your energy and you may have your own problems to handle. All I suggest is that you be realistic about what you can cope with, otherwise the failure of your relationship will just provide you with another scar.

Care – rather than possess, nag or dominate

Don't mix up loving someone with possessing them. Sometimes when we care a lot about someone we can get a little overbearing and this can turn into nagging and bossiness. I have a bad habit of thinking I know what clothes suit Tony best, but this is not my affair – if he wants to look untidy at the weekends, that's his business!

Before long helpful advice can become criticism and nagging. We all know what happens if someone nags us – we fight against the pressure and go even further down our own path. Sometimes love can take an obsessive turn and we can begin to want a person to be with us all the time, and to have their attention exclusively. This can lead to possessiveness and this brings jealousy, which questions trust and can quickly spoil a relationship. Try to overcome any tendencies to smother your partner. Let them have freedom – your worry about them will just envelop both of you with negative energies. You cannot be responsible for another person. You can only be responsible for yourself.

Sharing the same principles and ethics

Although you may have different spiritual beliefs I do think it is necessary for you to have the same attitudes towards people and the world. You can hardly be happy with someone who mistreats animals if you are an animal lover. You will struggle if you choose someone who doesn't hold the same loving attitudes as you do, who disregards the feelings of others, and is selfish and self-centred. If you decide to meditate every day don't dismiss your partner because they don't wish to join you, but realise that they may connect to God or the universe in their own way; but be wary of someone who is totally intolerant of your beliefs and ridicules them both privately and publicly.

Don't worry if your partner doesn't follow the same path entirely, although it helps if they are on the same side of the mountain!

ISSUES YOU MAY NEED TO TACKLE

Let's now look at some of the situations and questions that can arise with regard to our relationships.

Your friends are trying to pull you away from your partner

Circumstances may arise when your friends do not get along with your current partner. What do you do when your partner is not invited or your friends are encouraging you to leave your partner at home and come out with them on a Saturday night? If your relationship has any value you will put your partner first. You will, of course, see your friends and some time allocated to them is necessary for both of you, but if it is a matter of who has priority in your life – you are either with the wrong person or have the wrong friends.

If you positively prefer to be with your friends rather than your partner, then question if your partner is ideal for you. If you find you are following the wishes of your friends rather than your own feelings, then you may need to stand up to them or choose friends who support you rather than dominate you. Be strong and follow your own feelings, and be your own person.

I know of a young woman, a mother of two small children, who became increasingly frustrated with her husband and her restricted life. Her husband worked and she stayed at home and looked after the children. She had friends who would suggest that she came out with them during the day and sometimes in the evenings too. Her husband objected to the friends; he didn't like them or their ways.

The woman felt that as a matter of principle she should be able to choose her own friends and baulked against the criticism of her partner. She continued to spend time with her friends. Eventually, her husband gave her an ultimatum: either she would give up her friends or he would leave. She stuck to her principle of putting her friends first, and her husband left.

Over the next few months the woman nearly lost everything that she held dear in her life. She found herself increasingly in financial difficulties, missed the support of her loving husband, alienated her family and started to use drugs to alleviate the emotional crises that she was experiencing. Eventually, her strength of character pulled her out of the drug scene and she started to repair her life, but it has taken a long time – and it will take a long time for her to regain the trust of her partner. It is good to value and respect your friendships, but I suggest that you put your family and partner first in your list of priorities when there is a clash of interests.

Your partner has been unfaithful – what should you do?

If you and your husband truly love each other yet he slept with another woman – perhaps once on a trip overseas or a business seminar away from home – would you terminate your marriage? Would you forgive him his indiscretion, or would his unfaithfulness destroy your love for him? I suppose it will depend a lot on his attitude towards his action. It will also depend on your own attitude to unfaithfulness. If he is truly sorry for his misdeed and if you are a forgiving and tolerant person you may well let it go without visiting your lawyer.

Before you break up your marriage with righteousness decide whether the indiscretion was merely a momentary rashness or a flagrant abuse of your trust and love. Then follow your feelings – although you don't want to allow yourself to be emotionally abused and you certainly don't want to condone any treatment from your partner that will hurt you, neither do you want to destroy a good and loving relationship because of one slip-up. Generally speaking, men can have sex without it having a huge impact on their lives. There are many versions of the act of sex, from the cohesion of deep love to the satisfying of a passing desire.

Are you breaking spiritual laws by having an affair?

It is difficult to give advice on this subject out of context but generally we are living a lie when we have a love affair – we are certainly breaking trust and belittling the love of our partner. It usually involves creating a net of lies and therefore breaking the spiritual law of honesty. If we hurt and harm others, which can happen when we have an affair, we create a karmic reaction that will be detrimental to our happiness and peace of heart and mind. The stress that is normally attached to indiscretion will be equally damaging.

We may end up taking this path if we fall in love with a soul-mate while we are married to someone else. There may also be other factors involved, such as the long-term illness or disability of a spouse, or cultural ties that cannot be broken, which may mean that living a lie will be preferable to declaring love and destroying the emotional peace of others. In most circumstances, however, I believe that anything is better than lying day in and day out, and living with the deception and the fear.

Your partner isn't spiritual – what do you do?

This may mean that your partner doesn't want to go to workshops and meditation meetings with you. It may mean that they don't want to follow your particular spiritual path. I once asked a workshop that was full of women whether their partners were spiritual. They all said no, and that set off a discussion about how this upset them – and in fact some of them were considering leaving their partners for this very reason.

I then asked how many of the women considered their partners to be kind. They all put up their hands. I pointed out that being spiritual is not about meditating regularly, or reading the right books or going to workshops – it is about how you live your life and the way you treat others. The women all felt a great deal better once they had looked at their partners in this light, and all of them agreed that in fact they could describe their partners as spiritual because of their positive attitudes and loving ways. As I have said before, unless your partner is abusively against your beliefs, let them be and allow them to find their own way to God in their own time.

How do I know if I have met my soulmate?

Before we are born – between lives – we plan our next journey to Earth, and one of the most important decisions we make is choosing our partner. We may, in fact, choose more than one soul to come close to us and share our lives intimately at different stages of our life. We may have one special and favoured soul who has been with us on many of our physical manifestations, and there is a good chance that we will choose to meet up again.

When we meet someone with whom we have shared many lives we will feel an immediate bonding. We will feel we know them well, almost instantaneously. Have you ever realised very quickly that someone was going to be very special to you? Have you ever experienced that 'I know you' feeling on meeting someone? If the bonding is instant and strong, the chances are that you have met your soulmate – a friend and travelling companion of many lifetimes.

Soul energy can be divided, and many of us can be from the same energy source group. We may therefore have soul friends who are our soulmates, but don't necessarily come into our lives as lovers. They can be a dear friend, a mother, father, sister, brother or business partner.

At an early stage of its development, our soul is split, creating one female and one male soul. Our opposite gender soul is called our twin soul. You will have many, many things in common with your twin soul. You will most likely have the same spiritual aspirations and attitudes towards people and life in general. You will want the same things from life and have the same values. You may have very diverse interests, but your core values will be the same. However, even though you may marry or live with a soulmate or a twin soul, you won't necessarily have an easy ride, or a hugely successful coupling. You may have decided to challenge each other to help with your development, and the way your personalities have been affected by your genes could also result in a difficult close partnership. You will, nonetheless, have a deep bond that will be difficult to break.

Marriage

Marriage is an essential mainstay of all of the main world religions. Do we need it now? Of course, to be in a loving and supportive partnership it is not necessary to have a certificate from the government. However, I personally believe in the power of ceremony as a symbol of intent.

When we stand and say our vows to each other and to God, we are underlining our thoughts and intent. As thought and intent are the first stages of creation, I see a marriage ceremony as a beautiful way of acknowledging your feelings for each other, and a wonderful platform to show your intent to love and cherish one another and to continue to respect and support each other.

I feel that a ceremony shared with family and friends is a great endorsement of your commitment to each other. It is easier to connect to God in a place where the energies are pure and clear, and where others have shown their respect and love of God before, which is why churches and temples are great for such events. You can, however, perform your ceremony wherever it suits you to do so: indoors or outdoors, in a church, chapel, temple or garden. God will be there. You can use any form of ceremony that feels good for you – the essential ingredients are showing your love and respect for each other and your commitment to one another.

MEDITATION TO IMPROVE YOUR RELATIONSHIP

In this guided meditation you can use your intention to improve your relationship. You will be clearing away the negative energies that can develop between two people after they have been together for some time. Negative thoughts and attitudes can take people away from the closeness they experienced in the early days of their love. This is an opportunity to start afresh – to clear away the effects of the past. These are the negative traits you will be working on:

Jealousy	Anger
Distrust	Petulance
Possessiveness	Competition
Nagging	Criticism
Dominance	

✧ Find a quiet and peaceful location away from phones and other people.

✧ Sit comfortably and relax.

✧ Breathe in deeply several times, letting your heartbeat slow and your pulse quieten.

✧ Imagine you are in your personal healing garden.

✧ Spend a few moments walking through your garden and enjoying the beauty of the flowers, lawns, waterfalls, streams and pools with fountains and lilies.

✧ Follow a path that takes you deeper and deeper into the garden.

✧ You come now to an inner sanctum, a small, enclosed garden filled with pink roses. You are now in the garden of the heart, a place of great love.

✧ You see two benches facing one another and you sit down on one of them.

✧ Your present partner comes to sit on the bench opposite you.

✧ You see threads between your heart centres connecting you with love. These threads should be shining and pink but are dull due to the disagreements and negative emotions that have come between you.

✧ Make the intention to clear away these thoughts and attitudes and renew your love.

✧ Beside you are some golden scissors. Take these scissors and cut through the cords, releasing the negative energies as you do so as grey puffs of smoke – see them turning into light.

✧ Now envisage pure, light pink cords between you as you focus on the love you have between you.

✧ Determine to enforce your love with:

Tolerance   Compassion
Forgiveness   Support
Understanding   Freedom

✧ Sit for some moments and think about all the wonderful qualities that drew you to your partner when you first met. Think about the way you treated each other. Intend to find that unconditional and absolute love again.

✧ After you have spent time on this visualise yourself and your partner embracing, forgiving and loving one another.

✧ Leave the garden together, hand in hand.

On this romantic note we will leave our partners, boyfriends and companions, and turn our attention to our workplace and the challenges and opportunities that we face away from our home. We often have two faces – one for our friends and work colleagues, and one for home, where we can be more natural. When this is the case we have double the work to do if we want to achieve the smiley face that reflects our innermost feelings, and not a mask that we put on for the benefit of others.

Chapter Eleven

THE CHALLENGES OF THE WORKPLACE

I n your place of work there is yet another set of challenges that centre around your relations with your colleagues, employers and employees. We spend many hours in often stressful and pressurised situations, with people who we generally haven't chosen to be with in our lives (not consciously, anyway). There are any number of challenges that we must learn to face and handle, and many opportunities to walk the talk of our spiritual path.

ARE YOU IN THE RIGHT LINE OF WORK?

We had a look at choosing the right work in Chapter 1, so I will just touch on this subject here. It is, however, extremely important that you are the round peg, not the square one, in the round hole. There is nothing worse than struggling with a job that you are either not trained to do, or that is totally alien to your personality or skill base.

I hated my first job, but didn't know if this was just the nature of work and so stuck it out for a while. Fortunately, I was eventually able to move to another, slightly more appropriate job for me in the same organisation. I started as a typist/secretary for a bank manager. I was the world's worst typist, am numerically incontinent (I cannot hold a number in my head for more than three seconds), hated being tied to one place day in and day out, and had minimal shorthand skills. I experienced so many failures in this job that I would hide my aborted letters in my bag and take them out to the lavatory to flush them away, so that no one would see how many times I had to type a letter to get it right. Thank heaven for word processing and spell checkers. I really hated that job – I wasn't good at it and I wasn't happy.

This reminds me of two brothers I know. They ran a family catering business. The restaurant had been started by their parents, and when they were leaving school their mother became ill and they were asked to take over the business. One brother had planned to be an engineer and the other dreamed of being a farmer. Because of pressure from their parents both boys gave up their dreams and then spent over 30 years doing work that neither of them enjoyed. I wondered why they hadn't followed their dreams after their parents died, but they said it was too late then – they had got caught up in the groove of their life, and with families to support felt unable to change direction. They both found their allotted roles in the business stressful – what a terrible shame.

If you are in the wrong job you are putting yourself under great pressure and stress unnecessarily. You will be making yourself unhappy and all those around you will also be suffering – remember that the ripple effect works with negative energies too. Write down the following:

✧ ALL YOUR SKILLS *Examples*: good with people, good with children, good with animals, good computer skills, good manager, good No. 2, academic qualifications, technical qualifications, creative skills.

✧ WHAT YOU ENJOY *Examples:* working with figures, working with the public, caring for people, working with nature, challenge and deadlines, working for yourself, working on computers, working for a large and active corporation.

✧ YOUR IDEAL WORKING CONDITIONS *Examples:* indoors, outdoors, small office, being on the road alone, travelling overseas.

✧ YOUR ASPIRATIONS *Examples:* to be successful as a teacher or carer, to make a lot of money, to do charity work, to be the top of your tree, to change the world, to heal people.

Now look at your list – does it in any way match your work? Would you consider that you are in the right job? If not, start a plan to manage your way out of your present position and get to where you want to be. The first step in this change in your life is your *intention* to change. You have to release all thoughts that you are a victim of circumstance and realise that the person who can make this change in your life is *you*. Only you can make this happen – so do it.

If you are happy in your job and love it, good for you – well done, you are already following you intuition.

LACK OF APPROPRIATE TRAINING

One of the causes of unhappiness in the workplace is lack of sufficient training for the work you do. Your first step here is to be honest. Sometimes we don't like to admit that we are struggling, especially at work where any lack of confidence can be seen as a weakness or inadequacy. However, if you don't admit that you are in need of training it is likely that no one will offer it to you.

Find the training scheme you need, then ask if the management will pay for you to go on it. They may subsidise you if you are willing to pay part of the cost of it yourself. If you work for yourself or your company are unwilling to pay, then why not save up and put yourself through further training?

I have never regretted learning any of the skills that I have either taught myself or been taught, and it is amazing how some of these skills come into play when you least expect it. I taught myself to use a desktop publishing program when I was in Malaysia so that I could produce the expat newsletter. The skills I learned then have come into play over and over again for Hearts and Hands, which is the organisation I set up to assist others to develop their spirituality and healing skills. I have been able to produce flyers, workshop notes, newsletters and brochures because of my word-processing skills. I therefore believe that any skill that you feel drawn to acquire will be of benefit to you.

TOO HEAVY A WORKLOAD

One of the causes of stress and strain at work is being given too large a workload for the time available. You may counter this by working all hours, but this is not a good long-term solution. It will interfere with your home and social life, which you need to recharge, and it will ultimately affect your health. I have a friend who retired early mainly because of the excessive workload she was expected to cope with. Using the following list, check why you are not coping and see if the suggested solutions will help.

✧ You do not manage your time well.
   Tip: create a priority list and stick to it. Allocate enough time for all your tasks and use time slots.

✧ You spend too much time talking on the phone.
Tip: keep your calls short and sweet. People will get used to it in time and won't engage you in long, meandering conversations that gobble up your time.

✧ You spend too much time on the computer – answering emails or reading the spam.
Tip: put an anti-spam software check on your work computer or forward those lovely stories that lift your heart to your home email address. You can then spend as long as you like enjoying them outside of work.

✧ You want to help others so much that you listen to all the sob stories going in the office.
Tip: unless you are the welfare office, I suggest you give anyone who genuinely needs help your home number or the name and number of a therapist who you can recommend. You will be hurting yourself far more if you use your work time to heal and support those around you. Give them time during the lunch hour or after work, when you can concentrate on their needs.

✧ You cannot say no, so you are constantly overburdened with work.
Tip: if you have a choice about the amount of work you take on, learn to say, 'Sorry, but I am not taking on any more projects/files/leads.' Don't let your lack of confidence or the need to please be the cause of your overwork. Respect yourself enough to avoid making yourself a victim.

If you are definitely overworked through the greediness or lack of concern of your employers, then you have no choice but to confront them. Do this with confidence: tell them precisely and clearly what the situation is, and ask them to change it. If they do listen and are not prepared to accommodate you, think about changing your job. Your health is too precious to be completely exhausted by an ongoing, ridiculous workload. This is being self-responsible and honest.

Given that you are now in the right job or working on a plan to leave it, let's see what challenges the people you work with will produce.

JEALOUSY AND RIVALRY AT WORK

In most workplaces you are often in competition with your colleagues – and especially so if you are working in a sales office or in an environment where work standards are judged. Nothing inspires jealousy more quickly than the success of others when you are struggling with either your workload or your confidence. Actually, low confidence and self-esteem spawn jealousy more than work pressures do – if you are strong and confident about who you are you will not become jealous of another's success and will not see it as a threat to yourself.

If one of your colleagues is jealous of you, you may well feel this as a pain in the pit of your stomach or around the centre of your chest. This is where I pick up the energies of jealousy and envy. It is an uncomfortable feeling, and the best you can do is to go into your bubble, your protective egg, so that the emotions of your colleague will not affect you so much. You can also proactively send healing and light to them to help them lift above these feelings. They need healing to help with their own lack of confidence, and also with the discomfort of actually holding these negative emotions.

Most people do not want to be jealous – it is a feeling that comes over them unconsciously. If you are the one experiencing the jealous thoughts, you will know how they feel to you – maybe like butterflies in your stomach or a lurching sensation inside. It isn't pleasant for either you or the receiver of your jealous emotions – it also is followed by guilt, because you don't really want to feel badly about someone else's success. Here are a few guidelines to help you avoid the disturbing feelings of jealousy and other negative emotions that may arise at work.

✧ Work on your own self-esteem. Look for the cause of your low self-esteem and see if you can heal yourself with understanding and love. Perhaps you set your targets too high – maybe you are trying to be a perfectionist. Allow yourself to be as you are and love yourself for what you are and what you have achieved in life, rather than aspiring to achieve more.

✧ Intend to let go of the old emotions that have caused your low self-confidence by meditation and asking for spiritual help.

✧ Make a complete avowal to release the negative feelings. Do this at home in peace and privacy. Speak out loud the words, 'I am released of all negative thoughts and attitudes towards _____'

✧ Focus on the person, see how important success is to them and empathise with them. Put yourself in their shoes, and feel good for them. If it helps, see them as someone who desperately needs the good fortune.

✧ Whenever the feelings come over you, go to a quiet place and surrender to the light and let it fill you. This will replace the negativity within you with the lighter energies of love, making you feel calmer and more loving inside.

✧ Start a practical plan to improve your own self-confidence, self-approval and self-esteem. Make sure there are activities in your life that you can feel proud of. Do some charity work, help others, send healing to others – do something that will make you feel good and the issue in the office will fade away to insignificance.

✧ Is your jealousy caused by lack of attention from your employer and lack of recognition for what you have achieved? If it is, make a point of speaking out about your own achievements – obviously not too much or for too long, or you will become known as a braggart, but don't hide your light. I have seen situations where politically smart people have won the accolades due to their ability to project themselves well to the right people. You may not want to join in the political game, but if you work in the commercial or corporate world you should learn the skills necessary for your own survival. Telling management of what you have achieved is a form of honesty.

OFFICE GOSSIP AND BULLYING

One of the easiest ways for you to come off your path is to get involved in office gossip. The kind if gossip I refer to here is the running down of other people by a group. It's a little like bullying, really. One person is picked upon by the group and put under the microscope – then whatever that person does is talked about in a malicious way. The person can easily be made into a demon by those who are telling the stories and listening to them. This situation will get worse if the victim is not communicating. If you are the subject of gossip or bullying:

✧ Confront and engage those involved in conversation. They will de-demonise you once they know you a little better. You will become a person that they can empathise with and understand.

✧ Surround yourself with light (*see page 202*) every day before you go into the office.

✧ Acknowledge the bullies as weak people who are obviously suffering from either low self-esteem or emotional dysfunction caused by their past. Empathise with them; use your love and compassion to turn around the energies they are sending towards you. Send them love and light to heal their own pain.

✧ Hold yourself up high and show them that you are strong. From my experience bullies love to attack those they perceive to be weaker than they are, yet bullies are in themselves quite weak. See yourself as walking with armour around you – connect to the warrior role model energy (*see page 000*).

✧ Look for the good in the people who are attacking you; there will be something in their nature that you will find admirable. Focus on that – it will stop you from falling into the trap of hating and despising them. If you do go into negative thinking they will have, in a way, contaminated you also. Do your best to avoid this by concentrating on the best points in them and sending them love in your meditations.

✧ If you are being bullied by your boss confront them directly with this. Don't scream and shout, but do it when you are calm and in control of your emotions. You cannot be effective if you allow yourself to show anger. Say what the bullying is doing to you. Very often people do not understand the power they are wielding and the harm they do to others with their words. Point out the effects and ask them to contain themselves. If the bullying continues you need to take the matter higher. If you are reluctant to do this for yourself, do it for the sake of others.

✧ Be wary of joining a group to counter any bad behaviour from the boss or from colleagues. I have found that other people may support you in private, but once you take your objections and complaints into an open forum many people lose their convic-tions and 'bottle out', leaving you holding the flag alone. Groups also have different energies from individuals who feel strongly and have their own convictions – fight your battles.

If someone comes to you with gossip try to disengage yourself rather than joining in.

IRRITATING COLLEAGUES AND BOSSES

In a large office, there is no doubt that there will be at least one person who irritates you. Most likely that same person will irritate others as well. What can you do when such a person attaches themselves to you and apparently endeavours to annoy you whenever possible? What can you do without being rude? How can you handle this without hurting the person? Here are some suggestions for dealing with such situations.

✧ You know that what normally hurts and upsets people is how a message is delivered. If you swear and shout at someone they certainly get the message, but how is it going to affect them and what will it do for you? You may be able to release some frustration, but you are likely to feel guilty afterwards – I know I always do. So consider the other person's feelings and gently tell them that you are busy. Ask if they can please save all their questions and just come to see you once a week, or whatever the situation warrants.

✧ Perhaps you can allocate such a person a small time slot when you can give them your full attention – after all, most irritating people are looking for attention.

✧ Put yourself in your bubble of light and protect yourself from an irritating person's ways.

✧ If someone irritates you by speaking too loudly, whistling or annoying you and the rest of the workforce with silly jokes, loud laughing or other annoying habits, speak to them and ask them why they are so noisy. Of course, their answer won't match the true reason, but it will give them a chance to think about it. Maybe they don't even know that they are irritating. Almost without doubt, they will be seeking attention. So just do the best you can – see it as a challenge to your patience, tolerance and ability to keep your cool!

HOW TO HANDLE SOME TYPICAL WORKPLACE PROBLEMS

As I have said the workplace is a continuous challenge to your integrity and spiritual values. Here are some of the situations you may come across – remember to keep going back to the basic principles of your personal spiritual guide and use them whenever you are faced with a difficult decision or problem.

Company circumstances require you to make one of your staff redundant

Business problems and difficulties are simple to handle compared with personnel situations. They are by far the most challenging circumstances we have to face and deal with. This is a particularly difficult task because you are the bringer of bad news, and very often the person you are affecting will be harmed by what you have to tell them. They will suffer shock and will be traumatised by what you are about to do.

Speaking for myself, whenever I have been in any state of shock in my life, the way people have treated me has been critical and has left a lasting impression. Any kindness shown me when I have been down and vulnerable has stayed with me and comforted me since the event. So your kindness and the amount of attention you give to the interview will help the person afterwards. You cannot prevent the event, but you can do your best to give your understanding and compassion.

Don't tell the person you are delivering the news this, but I have to say that most of the people I know who have lost their jobs have found that it has worked to their higher good in the long run. This isn't the case for everyone, of course, but it is often an opportunity to change direction and it can propel us into a new life that we may be reluctant to start when we have a stable and well-paid job.

If you have any influence in the situation, it is a good idea to employ an agency that specialises in finding new positions for people in these circumstances. There are also counsellors who can help your employee and their family to come to terms with the shock of the situation and the longer-term effects both financial and emotional. Gather what professional advice is available to you on how to give the interview, and for the employee on what benefits, and so on, they will be able to claim and what help there will be for them either from the company or from the state.

Before the interview, meditate and ask for help – ask to be guided to say the right thing in the best way, and send light to the employee and their family. Pray that the greatest good will come out of the situation for them. Be prepared for emotion and be there for them – let them express themselves aggressively, fearfully or with sadness.

Conflicts of interest and loyalties in the role of a manager

If you are in any management position you will be faced with conflicting interests from time to time. Here are just a couple of examples of such instances.

Balancing work and domestic life

Although any employee may be faced with the problems of long hours and an invasion of their home and social time, it often becomes more inevitable when one is in a managerial or supervisory role. Getting the balance right is important for your domestic happiness and your work/business success. If you keep both in focus you will probably manage this balance; if you make sure you don't make promises you cannot keep to your partner, your children or your business associates, you can probably steer a path through the minefield. I suggest that you have sacred times that you reserve for your family, for example Sundays, children's nativity plays and sports days, as your business life is far more likely to encroach on your domestic life than visa versa.

Balancing the interests of the company and your employers against the interests and well-being of your staff
This can be difficult, especially if you are a team leader. You will have camaraderie with your group, which means that you will feel protective of them. Sometimes you may need to put the interests of the company or business before those of the individuals and the group. Trust your judgement and come from your heart when you work with these types of decision. Try to see the bigger picture, and if you feel that your employers are asking you to compromise your integrity and inner judgement too often, consider if you are working for the right company.

MAKING DECISIONS AND CHOICES AT WORK

Every day you will be faced with making moral and ethical decisions. Keep your spiritual guide near to hand and bring the values down to the lowest common denominator every time, for example asking:

✧ Am I being honest here?

✧ Am I doing this just for me?

✧ Do I feel good about this inside?

✧ Is patience or tolerance an issue here?

Do you avoid making decisions:

✧ Due to fear of reprisal or the consequences?

✧ Based on trying to impress or for egotistical reasons?

✧ With your personal gain in mind rather than that of the company as a whole?

✧ Entirely from a logical standpoint – allow your intuition to influence your actions?

Be big in your own shoes

One of the ways to gain respect in any job or walk of life is to be big enough to admit that you are wrong or don't know. I am always impressed with someone who is confident enough in themselves to apologise easily, and who can on occasions be prepared to take the blame for something that they didn't say or do, rather than cause a rift or disharmony and for the sake of the bigger situation.

Be prepared to say you are wrong or don't know

That is the way of the 'big character' – bluffing and lying are the way of the 'small character'. The first will make you feel stronger, the second inferior and weak.

Keep the bigger picture in your mind

Do this all the time, and don't let the small and insignificant issues cloud the picture. This sometimes means letting people get away with discrepancies and overlooking infringements for the good of the overall progress and well-being of a group, a situation or a project.

Your company's ethics

These days all companies of any size have a mission statement and a code of ethics. Take a good look at those of the business you are in and see if you feel good about them. You can also use these ethics as a backdrop to your everyday corporate and business decisions. If you don't approve or believe in the credo, or feel that the business has lost its way in following its own charter, consider moving on to work with people who can incorporate a spiritual aspect into business.

Anita Roddick successfully managed to set up a large corporation – The Body Shop chain, which manufactures cosmetic products – and incorporated ethical business practices and concern for the environment and people into the company. She demonstrated to a sceptical business world that you can include the highest of ideals and ethics in a corporate venture and still be successful and profitable. Her book *Business as Unusual* makes interesting reading and shows how she managed to walk the tightrope of big business and ethical trading.

The win-win concept

My dream is to set up a company that incorporates the full concept of the ripple effect so that every one in the chain is a winner. I would like the ethics of all corporations to be based on our spiritual philosophy of respect and consideration for all, where:

◆ Suppliers are not screwed so far down that they cannot pay their workers a decent wage.

◆ Labour forces in poor countries are used with respect and consideration.

◆ We ensure that the flow of money and commerce moves to all corners of the Earth, without restrictions and unfair advantages being given to groups of traders like the farmers and their subsidies in the EEC.

◆ The employees are treated with respect and encouraged to develop all their natural abilities.

✧ Employers take into account the entire labour force when they make decisions, and don't just look for a fast buck for the board members.

✧ Factory-placement and traffic-movement decisions take into full account the effect on the environment.

✧ Production is set up so that it is of the greatest benefit to the most underprivileged.

✧ A percentage of the profits can be passed on to help the underprivileged start small businesses of their own – empowering them and giving individuals and small communities a chance to grow.

I believe this will be the way of all companies in the future. After all, companies are the people who work in them, and if we are gradually changing everyone with our own personal inner transformations, then the ripples cannot fail to reach into even the largest of corporations.

I wish you well with your journey and thank you for the immensely valuable work that you will be doing to change the world to a better place for all. Remember that it starts with you.

I leave you now to continue on your journey. Remember that you are never alone and keep checking your guidebook. I hope we meet somewhere on the rock face, but in the meantime if you keep sending out the ripples – we will change the world!

Resources

BOOKS YOU MAY FIND HELPFUL

The Bible

Peter D'Adamo, *Eat Right for Your Type*, Century, 1998

Meher Baba, *Discourses*, Sheriar Foundation, 1995

Theolyn Cortens, *Living With Angels*, Piatkus Books, 2003

His Holiness the Dalai Lama, ed. Mary Craig, *In My Own Words*, Hodder & Stoughton, 2001

Alma Daniel, Timothy Wyllie and Andrew Ramer, *Ask Your Angels*, Piatkus Books, 1992

Harville Hendrix, *Keeping the Love You Find*, Pocket Books, 1993

Susan Jeffers, *Face the Fear and do it Anyway*, Rider, 1997

Anne Jones, *Heal Yourself*, Piatkus Books, 2002

Matthew Manning, *The Healing Journey*, Piatkus Books, 2003

Caroline Myss, *Anatomy of the Spirit*, Bantam, 1997

Michael Newton, *Destiny of Souls*, Llewellyn, 2000

Michael Newton, *Journey of Souls*, Llewellyn, 1994

James Redfield, *The Celestine Prophesy*, Bantam Books, 1994

Anita Roddick, *Business as Unusual: The Story of the Body Shop*, HarperCollins, 2000

Paul Roland, *Angels: An Introduction to Angelic Guidance, Inspiration and Love*, Piatkus Books, 1999

Antoinette Sampson, *Peace Angels*, Piatkus Books, 2002

Joshua David Stone, *The Ascended Masters Light the Way*, Windrush Publishing Services, 1996

Eckhart Tolle, *The Power of Now*, Hodder & Stoughton, 2001

Doreen Virtue, *The Care and Feeding of Indigo Children*, Hay House, 2001

Neale Donald Walsch, *Conversations with God*, Hodder Mobius, 1997

WEBSITES

Child Welfare Scheme Nepal:
www.childwelfarescheme.org

Regression therapist Janet Thompson:
www.janetthompson.org.uk

Hearts and Hands:
www.heartshands.org

Anne Jones:
www.annejones.org

Helen Barton, channel for John the Beloved:
Email: insight2@bigpond.com

The Ripple Organisation
www.make-ripples.com

INDEX

Note: page numbers in **bold** refer to diagrams

Hearts&Hands

Healing, Teaching and Support

Hearts and Hands is a non-profit-making organisation that is dedicated to spreading the understanding of healing for self and others. We have trained facilitators and healers throughout the world who can guide and support you to self healing and self empowerment. Hearts and Hands' services include:

- ❤ Distance Healing Network
- ❤ Telephone Help Line
- ❤ Meditation Group Network
- ❤ Children's Circle
- ❤ Energy Healing Sessions
- ❤ Workshops and seminars

For further information on these services and our overseas representatives please contact us at Hearts and Hands, 21 Honey Lane, Burley, Ringwood, Hampshire, BH24 4EN. You can visit our website www.heartshands.org and email us at care@heartshands.org.

R I P P L E

From one to another to the world

Ripple spreads the message of a new era of spirituality whereby individuals take responsibility for their own growth and healing. Our goal is to ignite the light within ourselves and facilitate its flow to others until the entire world is filled with Innerlightenment – the state of being where one is in touch with one's inner light and in harmony with one's self and the world. We provide knowledge, techniques and tools for the Innerlightenment of self and the empowerment of others through the Ripple Effect.

Ripple Products include:

- ♥ InnerScents – Essential oil blends, annointing oils, pure oils, massage oils, roller fragrances, room sprays. These blends hold the intentions of: *love, compassion, forgiveness, empowerment, healing, positivity, fearlessness, prosperity, patience, manifestation, freedom, synchronicity, divine connection*
- ♥ InnerCharms – Jewellery with the healing symbols that Anne introduces in her books and workshops
- ♥ InnerHealing – CDs of guided visualisations recorded by Anne
- ♥ InnerJourney – Seminars
- ♥ InnerPowerment – Corporate programmes

For further information on these products please contact Ripple at 21 Honey Lane, Burley, Hants, BH24 4EN, UK, email us on anne.jones9@btopenworld.com or visit our website www.make-ripples.com

For information on Anne's schedule and seminars please visit her website www.annejones.org. To contact Anne either write to Hearts&Hands or email her at anne.jones9@btopenworld.com